SUSSEX
CUSTOMS, CURIOSITIES & COUNTRY LORE

SUSSEX
CUSTOMS, CURIOSITIES & COUNTRY LORE

Tony Wales

Ensign
PUBLICATIONS

Published in 1990 by
Ensign Publications
2 Redcar St
Southampton SO1 5LL

Reprinted 1991

Publisher David Graves
Edited by Roy Gasson Associates.
Designed and typeset by PageMerger, Southampton.

British Library Cataloguing in Publication Data
Wales, Tony
Sussex: Customs, Curiosities and Country lore.
1. Sussex. Social life, history
I. Title
942.25

ISBN 1 85455 036 5

ACKNOWLEDGEMENTS

First of all I would like to record my appreciation of the authors of the many fine books on Sussex which have appeared over the years. I am particularly mindful of the many unsung heroes who slaved for love rather than material gain, in compiling histories of their own towns and villages. Without their dedication, our knowledge of this county would be much poorer.

Then I must mention with gratitude the many kind people, many of them unknown to me, who have enriched my understanding of past times in Sussex with their own personal recollections. Some of these most fascinating pieces of information have been passed on to me by members of the audience, after talks I have given to societies throughout the county.

Whilst it is quite impossible to mention all the folk who have contributed in different ways to this book, there are a number who I must single out for special thanks. Unfortunately some of these are no longer with us, but a mention in this list of acknowledgements may serve as a very tiny mark of my respect for their memory. To those who are still very much part of the present, I tender my acknowledgement of the help which in every case was so freely given.

Mr Barton of Rushlake Green, near Heathfield, Mr C.W. Cramp of Horsham, Mr W.J. Denman of Crawley, Mr R. Funnell of Slaugham, Mr H.R. Goatcher of Washington, Mr P. Jerrome of Petworth, Mr S. McCarthy of Crawley, Mr H. Mousdell of Ashington, Mr J. Norwood (Curator of Worthing Museum), Mr G. Townsend of Lewes, Mr C.E.J. Walkden of Rustington.

INTRODUCTION

My passion for all things connected with Sussex goes back many years – I can scarcely remember a time when my interest in the subject was absent. Even as a schoolboy I collected items connected with the county, forming my own small museum. (Its contents would be of little value today, so perhaps it is as well that I have no idea what became of them.) From teenage years onwards I collected books on Sussex, and my library now runs into four figures – in numbers of books that is, and not, I fear, in value (although many books which I see I bought for pence are now worth at least the same figure in pounds). I have also maintained notebooks and scrapbooks of newspaper cuttings over many years, and this material is of considerable help to me when writing articles and books.

This is not intended to be in any way a history of Sussex. You will not find accounts of great battles, famous families, or notable events, except perhaps in passing. It is, I hope, an intriguing treasure chest of curious lore and unusual scraps of information, much of it of minor importance to all but those of us who find anything connected with Sussex of abiding interest.

Please enjoy the book with the same sort of lighthearted enthusiasm with which it was written. And if you can add anything, or correct me on any aspect of fact, then please do not hesitate to do so.

CONTENTS

CONTENTS

Springs and Spas

One of the most pleasant memories of my childhood is of my "rich" uncle arriving on Sundays to take my family, and his own, on a picnic in the countryside. His favourite spot was just across the Surrey border, although I am not sure of its exact location. Here, beside a country lane, there was a perpetual spring, from which we drank with complete confidence. I can recall the particularly enjoyable taste of this water – it was quite unlike the tap water at home and it remained on our taste-buds for some hours afterwards, or so it seemed.

This was probably not a medicinal spring – the water was too sweet for that. But many such healing springs were known to country people, who made good use of them. Many of them had names with a Christian connotation, but often this merely overlaid a connection with a rather earlier form of belief or magic.

The chalybeate spring known as St Ann's Well, on the Wick Estate in Hove, was certainly in use long before it received the accolade of a saint's name. The unlikely story behind the name is that there was once a Lady Annefrida who was betrothed to a certain Wolnuth. While Wolnuth was away at the wars, Annefrida was noticed by Black Harold of Patcham Castle. When Wolnuth came home to claim his bride, the evil Harold had him killed. The body was buried amid the gorse at the scene of the murder and Annefrida wept so many tears over the grave that a spring appeared there. When she died, some years afterwards, she was buried near the same spot. Black Harold, repenting of his wickedness, surrounded the spring with stone and created a garden around it. The spring is said to be the starting point of a ley line that stretches over the Downs to Ditchling.

Dr Russell, who did so much to popularize Brighton as a health resort, recommended the spring to some of his patients, although the locals were already well aware of its properties. Mrs Fitzherbert was one of many notables who drank its waters and spoke in praise of it. Towards the end of the 19th century the conical roof over the well was replaced by a more elaborate well-house. St Ann's Well Gardens have been a public park since 1908, but sadly, the spring is no more and the well-house was demolished in 1935.

Petworth must once have been at least a minor place of pilgrimage – it had two shrines to the Blessed Virgin and, a short way from the town on the Fittleworth Road, the Virgin Mary Spring. The water from this spring has always had a reputation for healing, being thought particularly effective for eye problems. The water is said to be always warm in winter and cool in summer. The spring is used less today than in the past, but I am told that people still visit it occasionally, bringing a bottle to take some of the healing water home with them.

The first of Hastings' chalybeate springs was discovered in 1842 in the grounds of Hastings Lodge in Old London Road. It was said to contain nearly twice as much protoxide of iron as the spring at Tunbridge Wells. When a second spring was discovered at St Leonards, a man called Emil Grosslob saw his opportunity and opened a spa and Russian bath nearby. After a fire, the venture failed, and Hastings' brief period as a spa town came to an end.

More successful was Dr Peter Francis McCabe, who became Mayor of Hastings twice (1838 and 1843) and was a well-loved Alderman and Justice of the Peace. When, in 1846, the Fishmarket was almost wiped out by a very bad fire, he launched a

The Virgin Mary Spring near Petworth. *(Photo: P. Jerrome)*

Healing Waters of Sussex

relief fund for the fishermen. This was so successful that it paid both for their losses and for the construction of a well near Rock-a-Nore. A verse, quoted by Manwaring Baines in *Historic Hastings*, points to the paradox:

My Muse did once a joke devise,
And this a Doctor taught her,
That money raised because of fire,
Was well laid out in Water.

Dr McCabe seems to have been fond of water, because he also persuaded the local authorities to construct a small tank to receive spring water in St Andrew's Gardens (now part of Alexandra Park). This became known as McCabe's Well, or the Fairy Well.

In 1927, in the *Sussex County Magazine*, the Sussex archaeologist S.E. Winbolt told how he had helped to recover a piscina or water bowl carved out of a slab of sandstone, close to the village of Slaugham. Through a hole in the bottom of the bowl issued an inexhaustible supply of chalybeate water, known locally as a valuable eye lotion. Winbolt recorded that at one time a man came regularly from Horsham with a dog cart, bringing a barrel to fill and take back to the town; another man came from Brighton on a similar errand.

The local name for the Slaugham spring was My Ladies' Bowl, said to be because it was some ladies of the Covert family of Slaugham who, in the 17th century, caused the receptacle to be chiselled out, to keep the water clean and fresh.

Mr R. Funnell, who lives near the spring, tells me that for many years past his son and himself, as well as other locals, have from time to time cleaned out the bowl, which tends to become covered in leaves, twigs, and silted mud. Since the great storm of 1987, the area round about has become covered with fallen trees and it is now difficult to reach the spring.

The account of the Slaugham spring in the *Sussex County Magazine* brought forth another recollection from a reader in a subsequent issue. This story was of a lad who around the middle of the 19th century had suffered with his eyes, and, on the advice of Dr Hunter of West Hoathly, had bathed them with water taken from a chalybeate spring, known locally as the Holy Well, between Lindfield and Horsted Keynes. Reaching the spring was difficult, because of the boggy nature of the surrounding ground, so the accepted method of getting water from it was to cast out a bottle on a piece of string. The treatment in the case of the boy with eye problems was so successful that he enjoyed good sight for the rest of his life.

There are other magical springs around Sussex, but one more example must suffice. On my own doorstep, in Horsham there were once mineral springs that were used for medicinal purposes. Horsham has never been known as a spa town, but the waters from its springs were once bottled and sold by a local brewer. Now, of course, we buy our spring water from the supermarkets, and it comes to us from many miles away.

St. Ann's Well, Hove, before it was covered by a brick-built well house. The spring is now no longer in use.

Fairy Folk

Farisees (or "pharisees" – the spelling is optional) was the name given in Sussex to the fairies or little people. One man described these as "little creatures rather bigger than a squirrel, and not quite as large as a fox", another said they were "little folk not more than a foot high, and uncommon fond of dancing". The fact that Pharisees are mentioned in the Bible was considered proof of their existence.

There were, of course, fairy rings on the Sussex Downs. The author Arthur Beckett knew of rings that had occupied the same site on the Downs for several years. He noted that some measured many hundred feet in circumference, but most are much smaller. Gilbert White said that the secret of the rings is contained in the turf, and that grass taken to his garden from the Downs brought the rings with it. The true origin of the rings is in fact a type of fungus that throws its spores outwards so that a gradually increasing circle of greener and brighter grass is formed. Old country people, though, had a different explanation – they believed the rings were caused by the Little People, who were "uncommon fond of dancing".

Many Sussex place-names testify to the firmly held belief in the fairy folk throughout the county – Faygate, Pookbourne, Pook Hole, Pook-Ryde, Pook Hale, and Puck's Church Parlour, to name just a few.

Many superstitions connected with fairies existed. One of these concerned butter churning – once one of the country housewife's most trying chores. If the fairies held back the butter, the housewife would chant: "Come, butter, come. Come, butter, come. Peter stands at the gate, waiting for a buttered cake. Come, butter, come." The fairy often invoked at this time was Dobbs, or Master Dobbs, who was known for his kindness in helping with all kinds of household tasks. If you did more work than was expected of you, then you would quite likely be accused of having had Master Dobbs helping you.

As in other parts of the country, the Sussex fairies' colour was green, and this was considered a very unlucky colour for mortals to wear. (Even today a superstition against green as a colour for clothes is not uncommon.) The rhyme went: "Those dressed in blue have lovers true, in green or white, forsaken quite".

Probably the most magical place in Sussex is Chanctonbury Ring on the Downs. The fairies are supposed to haunt the Ring, along with the Devil and other spirits, but may be seen by human eyes only on Midsummer Eve, at midnight.

Sussex folklore is full of stories concerning fairies, some of them found also in fairy lore from other parts of the country. One of these stories tells of a ploughman who one day heard a little voice crying, "Help, help!" He asked what was the matter and the voice replied, "I have been baking and have broken my peel" (a little wooden shovel). The ploughman suggested it should be handed up to him so that he could repair it. This was done, and, with the help of a few tacks, the repair was effected and the tiny peel handed back through a crack in the ground to its fairy owner. When the kindly ploughman told his mates of the occurrence, he was met with smiling disbelief. But the next day, at the same time, he heard the little voice once more, and there in front of him was a tiny bowl full of some sweet-smelling liquid. It was so tasty that he quickly drank it all up, but when he put the bowl down, it slipped through his fingers and broke into little pieces. When he tried to explain the whole thing to his friends, he was again met with incredulity.

The most magical place in Sussex, Chanctonbury Ring, where the fairies dance on Midsummer Eve.

The Sussex Farisees

But the one who had laughed the loudest became ill, and died exactly a year after the event. Fairies cannot stand being laughed at.

Fairies, like witches, were interested in horses. A carter once noticed how fat his horses were becoming, and one night he hid in the stable to try to find out why. Soon he saw a group of little fairies appear, each of them with a bag of corn, which they fed to the horses. Suddenly one said to another "I twets, do you twet?" (sweat), whereupon the enraged carter jumped out of his hiding place and shouted "I'll make you twet afore I've done with ye". But before he could reach them, they had disappeared. Fairies never forget, and from that day onwards the carter's horses began to grow thin, until finally they were useless for work.

A similar story has the fairies threshing corn for the mortal. When one of the helpful fairies remarks that "he twets", the observer can contain himself no longer; he jumps out of his hiding place and shouts at the little folk in anger. Immediately he is struck by an unseen blow and from then onwards becomes an invalid, dying exactly a year later. Another tale of the rather dangerous help offered by the fairies tells of the Sussex farmer who found every morning that some of his wheat had been carried into the barn for him while he slept. Not being willing to let well alone, he kept watch one night and saw little men each carrying an ear of wheat upon his back. Once again one of them exclaimed "How I do sweat", and the farmer could not help himself replying "If you sweat for an ear, what would you do for a sheaf?". The touchy fairies immediately disappeared at this, and never contributed their help again.

Sometimes the blame for horses found in a sweaty state in the morning was put on fairies or the local witch. Probably the blame more rightly belonged to smugglers who undoubtedly often "borrowed" horses for their nocturnal enterprises. The folklore of fairies and supernatural spirits has often been invoked to conceal the activities of smugglers.

If you believe in fairies, you are in good company. William Blake, the poet and painter, once told a friend about a fairy funeral he witnessed during his stay at Felpham, near Bognor Regis. "The fairy creatures were the size and colour of green and grey grasshoppers, bearing a body laid out on a rose-leaf, which they buried with songs, and then disappeared". But somehow Blake's fairies seem to be rather daintier than the earthy and mischievous fellows of our Sussex traditions.

William Blake's cottage at Felpham, near Bognor. While living here he witnessed a fairy funeral.

Stamps, Cats, and Canaries

In these days of uniformity, it is pleasant to look back to some of the more individual houses of the past. In the last century some of our Sussex houses had as much character as their owners. For instance, at the time of Queen Victoria's Golden Jubilee, there was the Stamp House in the village of North Bersted, a couple of miles inland from Bognor Regis.

The originator was Richard Sharpe, who was the proprietor of the *Rising Sun* public house. For a wager he undertook to paper part of one room with stamps from his collection. But, as in many such enterprises, the whole thing took off, and within a short time the whole room – walls, ceiling, and even furniture – was covered in stamps. The complete operation took about five years, and Sharpe bought stamps by the thousand to supplement his own collection. The room was intended as a tribute to the Queen on her Jubilee and there were, of course, thousands of pictures of her – one on each stamp.

The fame of the room spread, and stamps began to arrive every day from near and far. Other parts of the house were covered in stamps, which were also threaded into "serpants" and hung from the walls and ceilings. (This idea of threading stamps with string through a hole in the centre was not uncommon at this time, and for ever afterwards has been the bane of collectors, to whom stamps so mutilated are valueless.) Others were arranged in the form of designs, such as Queen Victoria's likeness or the royal coat of arms, and then lacquered. The total value of the stamps used by Sharpe must have been immense. Eighty thousand pounds has been suggested as the cost to him of the project, although this sort of amount seems exceedingly unlikely. No one seems to know what happened to the stamps when the Stamp House closed down as an attraction for visitors.

As a boy in the 1930s, I heard about the Stamp House when I stayed with my aunt at Aldwick, near Bognor Regis. She gave me the impression that the house was still open to visitors, and as a keen stamp collector I hoped she might take me there some day. But by that time the collection must have been dispersed.

Sharpe died in Worthing Hospital aged 83, after a long illness, in the 1950s. All that is left of his brain-child are the picture postcards produced during the period when the Stamp House flourished, which now command good prices at sales and auctions.

Our second unusual house is at the quaintly named Pinchnose Green at Henfield, so called it is said because people pinched their noses to avoid the smell from the nearby tannery. The subject of our interest is the Cat House, which has below the eaves a charming collection of black cats playing forever with canaries in their paws.

The origin of this unusual form of decoration goes back to the 19th century, when the thatched cottage, which was originally known as Leeches, was the home of a Sussex eccentric, Robert or "Bob" Ward. Close by, in Martyn Lodge, lived Canon Nathaniel Woodard, the founder of the Woodard Schools. No love was lost between Ward and Woodard, and this discord came to a head when a cat belonging to the canon killed a canary owned by Ward. So that the outrage should not be forgotten Ward made black effigies of the cat, with a canary in its paws, and hung these around the house, rattling them by means of a string whenever the canon passed by. Not content with this, he arranged a jangling collection of scallop shells on wires, to add to the sound, and is even said to have fired off a battery of wooden cannons from his garden. He also made a hole in the cottage wall through which he blew a ram's horn whenever the canon passed – he called it his Zulu hole, presumably because he had fought in the Zulu wars. As a further eccentricity he hung flags and bunting from the trees in his garden. All this annoyed his other neighbours as much as it did the canon, and he was persuaded to moderate his protests.

This story may well have become exaggerated over the years – in fact it has been suggested that it was the invention of a journalist, and that the black cats were really hung around the house to keep birds off the peas. But let us not spoil a good story that now carries the respectability of time. Certainly there is little doubt that Bob Ward was a genuine eccentric. At some time in the history of the local church (probably its restoration in 1870) he acquired its altar boards, showing the Creed, the Lord's Prayer, and the Ten Commandments. These he used as the head and foot-boards of his bed, in which he slept until his death in 1891. After this they were rescued by the vicar and put back into the church, although not in the original site. In the course of time, too, the cats were resurrected in their present form and placed around the cottage, to form an unusual decoration that delights and puzzles many visitors every year.

Top: A good general view of the exterior of the Stamp House at North Bersted, near Bognor Regis. It was actually a pub, whose proprietor hit on this novel idea to increase the size of his clientele.
Centre: Inside the Stamp House stamps were hung in "serpents" on the walls, from the ceilings and even over the furniture.
Bottom: Henfield's Cat House as it was early in the 1900's. This was a picture postcard which was sold in local shops.

The Doctor's Tree

Crawley's best-known and most-loved landmark once stood proudly on the most northerly of the string of tiny greens that bordered the main road through the town. It was a specimen of the common elm, known to generations of Crawleyites as the Doctor's Tree. Local people boasted that it was nearly eight hundred years old and, although this may have been an exaggeration, no one could prove otherwise.

The tree got its name from a Dr Robert Smith, who in the 1790s took his bride to live in a nearby house, known as the Tree House. After the doctor's death, his son and succeeding generations of Smiths lived in the same house. Paving stones were laid inside the trunk of the tree, and Miss Mary Smith planted ferns, periwinkles, and other plants at the base. A rustic fence was maintained around the tree, and it was obvious that the Smith family looked upon it with great regard. When Miss Smith visited Ireland, she was delighted to find a small stationery shop selling pictures of the Crawley tree, although how they got there was a mystery.

When the tree was in its prime it must have been 130 to 140 feet high, but a picture of it in 1824 shows that by then the upper part had been torn away during a storm. It was, though, still of massive proportions, with huge lateral roots particularly on the east and northeast sides. The hollow bole at ground level had an inside measurement of about 35 feet, while the whole of the tree including roots had a circumference of 53 feet. These measurements were taken by Dr J. Martin (the "Father of Crawley") and Marcus Woodward. At the same period, a Gothic doorway led into a chamber nearly four yards across inside the bole. (Dr Smith had planted a young elm inside the original tree, but this failed to grow.) Although fenced to keep out undesirables, at different times the tree had been occupied by a poor wayfarer who gave birth to a child, by a family of vagrants who used it as a dwelling place, and by soldiers as a billet when marching from London to Brighton. The townsfolk also used the tree – as a meeting place, a convenient spot to hold town meetings, and even for tea parties.

At some period the chamber was used by the parish beadle as a lock-up. More happily, scholars of the church school assembled at the tree for their march to the rectory for their Easter hot cross buns. The tree was even mentioned in literature, being featured in Sir Arthur Conan Doyle's Sussex novel *Rodney Stone*.

Madame de Genlis, who visited the tree in 1823, recorded her impressions of it in the *London Literary Gazette* of 24 May 1823:

> *The tree, which is a great curiosity, is still standing in the village of Crawley, but as the Parish is not willing to be burdened with all the young elms that might be brought from the trunk of this singular tree, the Lord of the Manor has very wisely put up a door to the entrance of this lying-in hospital, which is kept locked up except upon particular occasions, when the inhabitants meet to enjoy their pipes and tell old tales in the cavity of this elm, that is capable of containing a party of more than a dozen. The interior of this tree is paved with bricks and in other respects made comfortable.*

Possibly because of the story of the vagrant who gave birth to an infant within the tree, it was commonly believed by young Crawleyites that the Doctor's Tree was where the doctor filled his bag with new babies before delivering them to their mothers.

In 1883 a September storm over the south of England caused great damage, and many of the limbs of the tree were torn away. By 1914 the attractive Gothic doorway had gone, but the chamber was reported to be still usable, although by then only about 10 feet high. By 1927 the height of the complete tree was said to be about 40 feet, including some new growth. A letter to the *Sussex County Magazine* in 1935 stated that a great gale had "demolished" the elm, but remains of the famous old tree were still in existence for several years after that before it finally disappeared for good. Now Crawley's famous tree is just a memory for the older townsfolk, and most of the younger ones do not even know where once, Crawley's babies came into the world.

Right: Crawley's famous Elm shown on a picture dated 1824, when it still has its Gothic doorway leading to a chamber within the bole.

Crawley's old tree, when it was still a familiar landmark, early in this century. Photo: Mr C.W. Cramp

Baked Mice and Spiders

A century ago a visit to the doctor was something not to be undertaken lightly. It cost money, when for working folk this was a very scarce commodity, and you were also considered something of a weakling if you sought help from a doctor for anything but the most serious illness. But there were always plenty of alternatives – in fact what today we would call alternative medicine was then the normal treatment. Herbs and flowers, even insects and animals, were used to provide the ingredients of the many home-made remedies in constant use. Most of them had some genuine benefit, and even today modern medicines still make use of some of the old materials, although we are not always aware of the fact. In some cases the old cures were accompanied by charms or some other kind of magic, which at least inspired confidence in the patient. There were also the plainly superstitious cures, which had no possible basis in any sort of medicine – but, such is human nature, even these often worked.

When writing about these old cures it is almost impossible to separate the genuinely medical ones from the magical, as the two often overlap. For a chesty cold, for instance, you were advised to cut a piece of brown paper into a heart shape, warm it, rub it with a tallow candle, and lay it on your chest. Would the cure have worked as well if the paper had not been cut into a heart shape? Probably not, if the patient did not have the same amount of faith in the cure.

Brown paper had the advantage of being cheap, and was used in several ways. For a bad back, a wife was advised to lay a piece of brown paper on her husband's lumbar regions and iron it with a hot flat-iron. One man was burnt by his wife in this way, and never dared to complain of back-ache again, in case she tried the same treatment. An old cure for toothache (and there were many) was to set light to a piece of brown paper, extinguish it, and inhale the fumes. My aunt, who had great faith in unconventional cures, was a great believer in this.

Rheumatism is still a very common complaint, but it must have been even more so when so many men had to work continually in the cold and wet, without a change of clothes, often doing repetitive work that required constant bending or stooping. Not surprisingly, then, we find many old folk remedies for the disease. A common belief was that if you carried something around with you – an unusually shaped stone, or more often, a potato – this would prevent aches and pains. Another rather gruesome belief was that an executed man's bones would do even better, and those taken from some poor wretch who had been hanged for murder and then exposed on a gibbet were much in demand.

Sometimes the ingredients used in folk remedies were unusual or scarce, but more often they were common objects available to everyone. Many old cures made use of such things as apples and onions, plantain leaves, stinging nettles, or pulped potato – the last as an ointment for burns. Most of these were, of course, perfectly sensible, and were as likely to work as the medicines we nowadays obtain from the chemist. But what can we make of cures that utilized mice, spiders, shrews, and snakes? The idea that the more unpleasant a thing is the more it is likely to work must have been very common in the past.

Mice, baked and eaten with onions, were suggested as a cure for whooping cough. (Another cure was any remedy prescribed by a man riding a piebald horse.) Mice baked to a cinder, powdered, and eaten with jam were a sure cure for bed-wetting in children; dried and powdered, they were a remedy for diabetes.

A live spider rolled up in butter and swallowed was said to cure jaundice. I can think of scarcely anything worse, although I once heard of an old gardener who would pop a certain type of spider into his mouth as a delicacy, when wandering round his garden. Another use for a spider was to swallow it wrapped in its own web, as a cure for ague, a kind of malaria once much more common than today. A little less distasteful was the use of the spider's web by itself, as a quick and easy way to staunch blood from a cut, even a very bad one.

Shrews used to be considered bringers of evil. Lameness in a cow was sometimes attributed to a shrew running over the animal's foot. To cure this, a shrew-ash was made. A hole was made in an ash tree and a live shrew inserted and sealed in. A twig from the tree, rubbed on the affected limb, would cure the lameness.

Warts probably inspired more home cures than any other problem. The most popular cure was to rub the wart with a piece of raw meat, which was then buried (or, in more recent times, flushed down the loo). Warts may also be made to disappear by wishing them on to someone else, surely a most anti-social act, or by selling them – although I am not sure who would be willing to buy them. As a last resort there was always the wart-charmer – a sort of white witch (male or female) who had the power to remove warts at will.

Charms, often a mixture of Christianity and magic, were written out on pieces of paper and sold at fairs. Sometimes those who bought them could not even read what was written on the paper, but they still had faith in the power of the charm. For a burn the following was considered efficacious:

Two angels from the North,
One brought fire, the other brought frost,
Out fire, in frost,
In the name of the Father, Son, and Holy Ghost.

Ague, much dreaded, could be cured by this charm:

Ague, ague, I thee defy,
Three days shiver, three days shake,
Make me well for Jesus' sake.

And for a wound caused by a splinter or thorn:

Our Saviour Christ was of a pure Virgin born,
And he was crowned with a thorn,
I hope it may not rage or swell,
I trust in God it may do well.

And finally a general charm for all occasions:

Ye three Kings; Caspar, Melchior, and Belthasar,
Pray for us now and at the hour of death.

George Attrill of Fittleworth. The shelves of his cottage held several home made cures, including an ointment made from Adder fat, which was good for ear-ache and several other complaints.

Everyday and Sunday Best

One of our few truly English folk costumes, the country smock, or round-frock, was originally part of the countryman's daily garb in Sussex as in other parts of the country. Even after fashions had changed and the smock had become out-dated for everyday wear, it was still worn by bearers at funerals and for events such as Club Days and marbles championships.

Battle Museum has an 1838 smock labelled a "Sunday or Funeral Smock". At the funeral of the Rev. John Goring of Wiston House, in around 1895, the coffin was carried by employees of the estate wearing brand new smocks presented to them for the occasion. As late as 1928 smocks were worn by the six bearers at the funeral of Mr Vernon Musgrave at Kirdford. At least up to 1958 there were eight white smocks kept at the blacksmiths at Warbleton, to be worn by bearers at funerals.

Smocks were worn on happier occasions, too. They lasted at annual village Club Days until the 1920s, although at Harting the number to be seen each year dropped from about fifty late in the 19th century to just one or two by the early 1900s.

Choirmen at village churches also wore smocks on Sundays. In the last century it was a common sight to see the men of the church choir at Warnham sitting on the gravestones in the churchyard before the service, wearing their smocks and smoking their clay pipes. The Warnham parish clerk and fiddle player, Michael Turner, who was born in 1796 and appointed clerk and sexton in 1830, always wore a smock when carrying out his duties.

When the Sussex squire John Fuller presented a barrel organ to Brightling church, he also gave each male member of the choir a new smock, which was worn with buckskin breeches and yellow stockings. (The women were given red cloaks.)

Obviously, then, there were two kinds of smock – the serviceable everyday working garment, often termed a round-frock, and the more dressy Sunday version, worn as a mark of distinction. A few years ago correspondents in a Sussex magazine carried on a lively debate on the difference between the names "smock" and "round-frock", but nowadays the two terms seem to be used indiscriminately.

It is no wonder that smocks were popular as working wear in Sussex – they were windproof, yet cool in summer, and could, by dipping, be made almost waterproof. They are, as I can testify, extremely comfortable. Shepherds invariably wore them, buying them at the September Fair at Lewes, along with their big umbrellas and other shepherding gear.

Although white smocks were most popular for ceremonial occasions, work smocks could be in a variety of colours. Some colours were the badge of certain trades – carters and ploughmen wore black or grey and shepherds sometimes wore blue.

By the early part of this century smocks were disappearing fast. They were everyday wear only for the older men whose wives hadn't yet managed to persuade them to give them up. The Sussex author Arthur Beckett complained that he walked sixty or so miles through the Downs in 1909 and spotted only two men wearing smocks. Even in 1889, Lady Hurst found it sufficiently unusual to comment on an old man in a white smock who was to be seen each Sunday in Horsham parish church.

It was said that the smocks were usually cut out by the men, although made by the women. All smocks had in common the familiar absence of curves and all used the full width of material in the body but the design of the smocking and the length of the garment varied tremendously. Some old photographs show very short garments, and it has been suggested that trades such as carters might have preferred these, although other photos do not bear this out. Probably it was all down to the personal preference of the maker or the wearer, or perhaps even to the amount of material available. One lady whose father wore his brown linen smock on Sundays when he made his regular round of the farm, remembered that he always wore it rolled up to just below his waist, to avoid making it dirty.

There were unexpected advantages in wearing a smock, or so the old Sussex humorists would have us believe. At mealtimes you could catch table scraps in it to eat later at leisure. When trying to catch a runaway animal, such as a pig, you could sit on your heals and persuade it to run into your smock.

We will let William Cobbett have the last word on Sussex smocks. He stopped at Billingshurst and notes, in *Rural Rides*: "A very pretty village and a very decent public house. Landlady sent her son to get some cream, and his main garment was a blue smock-frock faded from wear and mended with pieces of new stuff, not faded. Just such a chap as I was at his age."

Sussex smock showing the beautiful smocking which was worked on some of these garments.
Photo: Courtesy Museum of English Rural Life, Reading

Labourer in black Sussex smock in 1880, outside Bignor church.

Jacob's Post

In 1734 Jacob Harris, a travelling pedlar, murdered Richard Miles by cutting his throat and stole his victim's riding coat, valued at 10 shillings. The attack took place at a wayside inn on Ditchling Common on 26 May, although Miles did not die until 30 May. Harris, who was also known as Jacob Hirsch, fled after the deed to Turners Hill, where he was arrested and taken to Horsham Gaol. At the next Sussex Assizes, held at Horsham in August 1734, he was indicted for murder and condemned to be hanged. On 31 August the sentence was carried out, and Harris's body was hung in chains on a gibbet near the spot where the murder had been committed.

As was often the case, a ballad giving all the gory details of the crime and subsequent execution was quickly concocted and put on sale. The ballad is too long to give in full, but here are the final lines:

And where he did the crime they took the pains,
To bring him back and hang him up in chains,
That there he might be seen by all that passed by,
I wish all people who will cast an eye;
It is a dismal sight for to behold,
Enough to make a heart of stone run cold,
So to conclude I hope you will take care,
And of all wilful sin, I pray, beware;
Let's serve the Lord with all our might,
And he will guard us day and night.

What finally happened to Harris's bones we do not know, but at some time after they had disappeared a post was erected on the site of the gibbet as a reminder of the crime. It bore the date 1734 and was surmounted by the figure of a rooster. On several occasions this post was renewed, although most people seeing it probably always thought it to be the original. At one period the post had a neat fence around it. There is still a replacement post standing today, although a portion of what is believed to be the original is preserved not far away.

The memorial was, even as recently as the late 19th century, credited with magical curative properties. It was not uncommon for people to come from several miles away to obtain a piece of Jacob's Post, which they would carry with them at all times to ward off ills. It is probably because so many pieces of wood were hacked from the post for this purpose that it had to be renewed from time to time. Presumably the metal work on the top was never damaged and so could be re-used whenever the wooden section had to be replaced.

It has been said that this, the only memorial of its kind in Sussex, commemorated the last occasion when a man hanged for murder was exposed to the public gaze after his execution. But Harris was not, in fact, the last murderer to be so exposed. John Breads was hung in chains on Gibbet Marsh after he was executed for a murder at Rye in 1743. The chains are now in Rye town hall. Even more memorably, in 1793 two men were hanged and gibbeted near Old Shoreham Road, Hove. It was this event that inspired Lord Tennyson to write his sombre and moving poem "Rizpah", in which the mother of one of the executed men bewails the loss of her son and the fate that has caused his mortal remains to be exposed to public gaze. As the poem says, "They hang'd him in chains for a show...".

Jacob's Post was supposed to be haunted and local folk were not keen to pass it after dark. One night a drinker at a local pub was dared to go and stand by the memorial at midnight. Unknown to him, one of his mates had slipped out first and hidden himself nearby. When the decidedly nervous hero got to the spot, he did his best to keep up his courage by talking to the ghost: "Hello Jacob, how are you tonight?". From the shadows came the quivering reply, "Very wet and cold". The poor man turned and ran, and didn't stop until he had gained the safety of the bar parlour and was again surrounded by his friends. When the joke was explained to him, he failed to appreciate the humour of it – although it kept the regulars at the pub entertained for weeks.

Above: The chains in which a murderer was hung and exposed to public gaze at Rye in 1743.

Left: Jacob's Post on Ditchling Common, topped by the metal figure of a rooster and the date of the murder 1734.

Gentle Giants

Piddinghoe folk once used to amuse their visitors with a riddle: "Where do they shoe their magpies, and hang their ponds out to dry". The answer was, of course, Piddinghoe itself, because here they dried chalk from the ponds and shoed their black oxen.

Not that oxen were always black, or even always shod. In Sussex they were as likely to be the dark red beasts that were used on the Downland farms, and they were taken to the blacksmith to have shoes fitted only when it seemed absolutely necessary. Shoeing oxen was a task that most blacksmiths and their helpers heartily disliked. Oxen were not as obliging as horses – they had to be thrown and their legs secured for the operation.

No one seems to know why oxen went out of favour on Sussex farms. Up until the 1920s they were still being used, and they fell out of favour not because of mechanization – horses, after all, were still in regular use – but merely, it seems, because of a change in farming fashions. At about this period a picture postcard was produced showing "the last team of oxen ploughing in Sussex", but it is in fact extremely difficult to decide for certain which was the last team in regular use. A writer in the *West Sussex Gazette* in 1978 thought the last team to have been that owned by Major Harding, a gentleman farmer of Birling Manor Farm. This team was still ploughing at East Dean in the 1920s, when the local post office sold a penny postcard showing them at work. Mr Gorringe's farm at Exceat has also been claimed as the Sussex farm on which oxen last worked. Arthur Beckett, in his *Adventures of a Quiet Man* (1933), has a chapter on Sussex Ox Teams in which he mentions that both Major Harding's team (which he calls a "revival") and Mr Gorringe's team (a "survival") were still working in 1924. He also starts the chapter by saying that "Farmer G. has decided to sell his ox team, the last or almost the last relic of the farming methods of the hill farms of a generation ago". Presumably he meant Mr Gorringe.

Edward G. Martin in *Life in a Sussex Windmill* (1921), mentions some oxen sold at auction in 1912 and described by the auctioneer as probably the last working oxen he would ever sell. Two pairs were bought by Mr Scarse, and two pairs by Mr Elphick, but it is not clear whether these were to be used as working beasts.

Obviously working oxen were becoming unusual in Sussex by the 1920s. Mr Thomas Mills of Cowfold recalls that up until World War I a cart pulled by oxen travelled each week from Cowfold to Horsham market. *The Field* of 19 November 1925 pictured a team of six oxen ploughing, with a caption stating that this was one of the last teams ploughing on the South Downs "this Autumn". What must be one of the final sightings of an ox team ploughing was recalled by Mrs Winifred Wadsworth, who told me that when she was 15 in 1927, she watched a man ploughing with two oxen on the Downs near Lancing. This was evidently sufficiently unusual for it to have been retained in her memory.

To go back to even earlier times, Mr E.G. Apedaile, writing in 1936, recalled that oxen were used regularly for ploughing in the Horsham area in the 1870s. He remembered those belonging to Mr R. Aldridge of St Leonard's Park being shoed at Ethertons, the blacksmiths at the corner of Springfield Road. These premises were later taken over by Stephens, the ironmongers, and when they eventually closed down a lot of old stock was turned out and sold off. Among this stock was a box of metal objects labelled "oxen nails". Apparently they

"The slow, black oxen toiling through the day."

A team of black oxen (or "magpies" as the riddle had it) working on a Sussex farm early in this century. They were used for all kinds of tasks, in fact anything that a horse would otherwise do.

Working Oxen in Sussex

had remained undisturbed in the stock for around a century.

The ox teams were usually controlled by an ox-boy, who used a long pole called a goad. Its length was 8ft 3in and it was used as a measuring rod on the farms. Driving a team of oxen was not an easy job, and the only means the ox-boy had of enforcing his will on the huge beasts was this thin hazel stick, which had a piece of wire about an inch long projecting from its business end. Armed with this, and a few well-chosen phrases, the driver could manage his team with considerable dexterity.

Not everyone enjoyed working with oxen. George Townsend told me some of his memories of teams of "bullocks", as he called them. At one time he was working for his father, who was bailiff of two farms owned by the Earl of Chichester at Falmer. One day the oxman was ill and George was asked to deputize for him. The team was of eight oxen, although as a rule only six were used at one time, as the soil was light. George said: "I had a fortnight. I had quite enough of oxen in that time. Horses for me. Oxen were very ignorant, not like horses who seem to know what you say to them when they get used to your voice".

Although horses were undoubtedly the more intelligent, oxen were not entirely devoid of sense, and those who worked with them continually were quite happy with the relationship they had with their charges. They were given names, such as Turk, Tiger, Hawk, or Pheasant, and would be quite capable of answering to their own name when being yoked to a wagon or plough. They were prepared to be obedient to their usual ox-boy, but appeared dull and unwilling to anyone else.

Their great advantage was in their ability to pull strongly and steadily without needing a breather. In 1887 a steam threshing traction engine became partly submerged in a pond near Saddlescombe. A team of six oxen was yoked to the machine and easily pulled it out. The classic example of the strength of oxen though is the well-documented occasion in 1797 when 86 oxen were used to haul a complete windmill a distance of two miles from Regency Square to Dyke Road, Brighton. Oxen had another advantage over horses – they thrived on a cheaper diet and when their working days were over, they could be fattened for beef, fetching good prices.

But even these attractions were not enough and the sight of a team of these gentle giants working in the Sussex fields had disappeared completely by the 1930s.

A team of oxen working on the Downs near Lewes. The ox-boy has his "Goad", a thin hazel wand tipped with a sharp point, with which he controlled his charges.

Photo: Courtesy Mr J. Parkhurst

Grave Stories

Funerals in the 18th and 19th centuries were often very elaborate affairs, particularly if the person most concerned had been well-to-do. Sometimes the ceremony was carried out at night with a torchlight procession, although this seems to have been accorded only to the very rich. Miss Elizabeth Gatford, a noted Horsham eccentric, was buried in this way in 1799. The Rev. Evans from London preached the sermon, and the chapel and burial ground were crowded with her friends and other curious folk, in spite of the hour. The last night-funeral in Horsham – of Mrs Killick of Tanbridge – took place in November 1829. The church was illuminated entirely by candles.

Although nowadays we associate black with death, this was not always the case. The bearers at many funerals in past centuries wore their best white smocks – in fact, funerals were probably the last occasions when smocks were worn by men as a matter of course, some time after they had gone out of everyday use. Sometimes it was the women who wore white. In 1798 a journeyman carpenter was buried in Salehurst churchyard, with the pall being supported by six young women dressed in white.

Paupers from workhouses were buried with little ceremony. A letter to the *West Sussex Gazette* in 1865 asked why Petworth workhouse did not have the use of a plain hearse, after the writer had witnessed a poor person being carried to the churchyard in a pony cart. It was a common sight to see a corpse being brought to the graveyard for burial in a farm wagon.

Sometimes, though, the poor benefited from the funeral of someone in more affluent circumstances. In the 18th century it was the custom to give black hatbands and gloves to relations attending a funeral, and loaves, money, or gloves to the poorer folk, as happened at a funeral of a shopkeeper in Brede in 1762.

When a Sussex shepherd was buried, a tuft of wool would be placed on his coffin so that St Peter would know what his job was and understand that he had been unable to attend Mass as often as he might have wished. Sailors drowned at sea and recovered on Sussex beaches were buried beneath circular grave mounds. The reason for this strange custom is not apparent.

In 1933 George Aitchison enquired in *Sussex Notes and Queries* whether other Sussex parishes followed the pleasant custom of a certain West Sussex churchyard, where children's graves were placed near to the pathway. The reason given was that the children would not feel lonely if they were close to the path where their friends would be passing by.

Even when dealing with a sombre subject such as funerals and death, the dry Sussex sense of humour was not completely absent. Miss Faith Woods was told a good story by her father. The Slinfold village simpleton was walking home late at night through the churchyard, talking away to himself as usual. Some of the village bloods decided to play a trick on him, and one lay flat on a tombstone as he approached, repeating over and over in plaintive tones "I can't get in, I can't get in". After a moment's reflection, the idiot gave the trickster a mighty whack with a spade, exclaiming loudly, "You old silly, you've no business out".

Another rather similar story was told to me by Mr Jim Laker, who was brought up in Worth. The churchyard there is said to be haunted, and one New Year's Eve one of the village youths decided to frighten the bell ringers. He dressed up in a long white nightdress belonging to his mother, and covered his face and hands with flour. "Who do you rackon that is then?" asked one of the ringers conversationally. His companion, who was also the gravedigger, gave the question some consideration and then replied "I dunno, but it aint one of mine, I allus dig mine in praper".

There are many such stories, trotted out by the oldsters over their beer, when the right kind of audience is listening. A rather grimmer one is the tale of a well-known, local unbeliever who accepted a bet to spend a night in a church that had the reputation of being haunted. When challenged that he might not actually turn up to carry out the bet, he promised to drive a large nail into the wooden floor of the church, as proof that he had been there. In the morning he was found dead of fright, still kneeling on the floor of the church, held firmly by the nail he had accidentally driven through his smock.

Top right: Funeral procession of Captain Collins, 4th September 1912. Typical of the sombre ceremonial observed at such funerals around this period.

Right: Funeral of Mr Napthale (Nap) Page leaving Perching Manor Farm for Edburton Church in 1912. The coffin is on a hand-drawn bier, followed by the horse who was Nap's favourite hunter. Photo: courtesy Mr J.R. Thomas

"Me and My Little Barrel"

The village inn served lots of purposes – as a social centre (for the men), as a headquarters for the friendly society, as a place for rents to be paid and legal scores settled, and much more besides. But its main purpose was to sell refreshment of an alcoholic nature and the main occupation within it was drinking. Toasts to accompany the drinking were often recited – indeed they seem to have rolled off the tongues of regular drinkers with very little need for thought. One of the most common toasts was:

Here's to me and my little barrel,
And I wish that we may never quarrel.
But if we do, it will be the time,
When its belly's empty, and so is mine.

A simple philosophy for life, even more definite in this next one:

Bread when you're hungry,
Beer when you're dry,
Bed when you're tired,
Heaven when you die!

Or this:

Here's to three B's and an H,
Bread to eat, Beer to drink,
Bed when you're weary,
And Heaven at last.

But it was not always so idyllic. The cost of the beer sometimes robbed the family of more essential items:

Good drop of beer I love you,
You robs me of all my clothes,
But good drop of beer I love you,
As down my throat you goes.

Similar sentiments are spelt out even more clearly in this one:

Here's to beer I love thee, In thee I put my trust.
I'd rather have a bellyfull than go to bed athirst.
You've kept me in bad company,
And kept me from good clothes,
But with all my heart I love you,
So down my guts you goes.

There was often quite a lot of social comment in these toasts, and a very definite yearning for things to be absolutely perfect:

Good beer a year old, good bread a day old,
Good beef, hot or cold, and a good wife
who'll never scold.

But sometimes the sentiments were a little more forthright:

Here's to those that wish me well,
And those that don't can go to Hell.

Some toasts were quite long. One that starts "Here's to the man with the ragged coat" goes on for 26 lines, ending with a poem sometimes known as "The Farmer's Creed". This concludes with the lines "God Speed the Plough, Here's Long Life and Success to the Farmer". These or similar words were often inscribed on two-handled mugs, together with a coat of arms showing the farmer and a dairymaid with the tools of their trade. Although there is nothing peculiarly Sussex in these mugs, we do have our own pottery – Rye Pigs and Brede Hedgehogs, for example. The Rye Pig was a little jug (the body of the pig) and an even smaller cup (the head). A drinker could use the cup and claim that he had imbibed a "hogshead" of ale unaided. Speaking of Sussex pigs, there were some even smaller ones made of brass, with the tail in the form of a ring, so that the little animal could be hung on a watch chain. The head hinged back, and the body held small matches that could be struck on the belly of the pig. I am told that butchers were particularly fond of these.

Rhymes and inscriptions on mugs and jugs are not uncommon, and some interesting ones may be

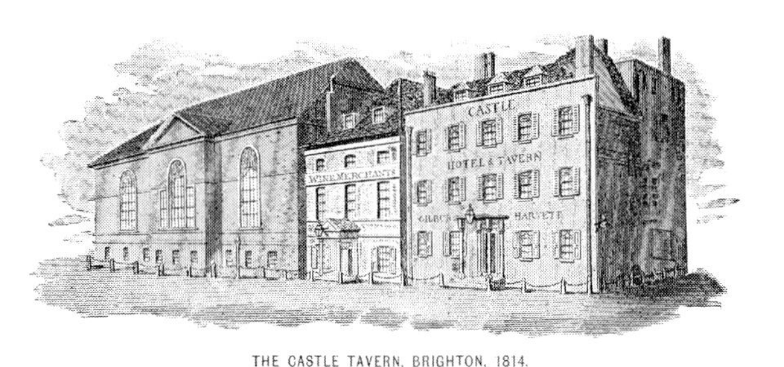

THE CASTLE TAVERN, BRIGHTON, 1814.

found in Sussex pubs. An old mug found in the chimney of a Horsham house contained some money and bore the following inscription:

Hard very hard,
The life of man is but a span,
But a woman's life a yard.

More revealing is this rhyme on a spirit flask:

A little health,
A little wealth,
A little house to live in,
And at the end,
A little friend,
And a little cause to need him.

The mug owned by a well-known Sussex miller carried the following piece of doggerel:

On Highdown Hill there stands a mill,
The miller is honest you will find,
For he takes toll from both great and small,
Who send him their corn to grind.

And, lastly, a very apt rhyme on a punch bowl from Chailey:

Fill your glasses lads and lassies,
Round the maypole frisk and play,
Smiling, glancing, singing, dancing,
This is Cupid's holiday.

If it seems that this section has included far too much in praise of drink and drinking, consider how much more sober the 19th century was than the 18th. In 1798 an old woman of Lewes, over a period of nearly five years, drank 2,280 drams of rum out of the same glass at one public house – and this in addition to what she may have drunk elsewhere!

Country pubs offered annual events such as feasts and fairs, to boost their custom. This was the Strawberry Feast at the Frankland Arms, Washington on 4 July 1906.
Photo: Mr and Mrs J. Sykes

An undated photo from Shoreham, given to me as an interior of an inn. The lack of drink plus the religious texts on the walls, makes it look much more like a social club – possibly for local fishermen. *Photo: Courtesy W. Truscott*

Cock and Hen Stories

Cock fighting has a very long history and references to "cocking", as it was called in Sussex, abound in the county's literature.

As early as 1746, cock fighting was taking place in Brighton, and it continued in the town for many years. A typical advertisement read:

Cocking
To be fought, a Day's Play, on Thursday next, the 16th inst., at the Castle, Brighthelson, for four guineas, a Battle, and Ten the odd Battle. To begin at Eleven o'clock. NB: Dinner to be on the table at two o'clock precisely.

At Lewes in 1778, cockfighting was advertised in the *Sussex Weekly Advertiser* in these terms:

Cocking
To be fought, on Thursday the 25th inst., at the Swan, in the Cliffe, a Day's Play of Cocks, between Gentlemen of Lewes, and the Gentlemen of Newhaven, for 2 Guineas a Battle and Five the Odd. A pair of large cocks to be fought before dinner. NB: Dinner to be on the table precisely at One o'clock.

The similarity of the wording of these two advertisements would make it appear that at this time there was a formal code established for the ordering of such events.

Cocking was sometimes accompanied by other equally cruel sports. A Sussex newspaper of 1810 reported: "On Monday, the Easter Holiday folks, in all the brilliance of Sunday finery, assembled in great numbers at the Bear public house, about a mile north of the town, on the grounds contiguous to which they were subsequently entertained with the polished diversions of cock fighting, and the baiting of a badger". One wonders what was considered "polished" about such diversions.

Henry J. Smith, writing about Southwater as it was in 1907, said that once, when there was a cockfight at the Cock Inn, a boy from Shipley who was on his way to Horsham to buy a pair of breeches stopped to enjoy the fun. He could not resist betting his only half-crown and as the fight went on he shouted "Breeches or no breeches". The cock he bet on was the winner, so he shouted "Two pairs of breeches".

Tales of Old Petworth was written largely by John Osborn Greenfield (1802-69), and rescued from oblivion by my old friend George Garland, the well-known Petworth photographer. The tales were published in 1976 and tell us a tremendous amount of how things went on in a Sussex country town in the early part of the 19th century. The details about cock fighting are particularly revealing. We are told that the champion was usually brought to the scene of battle in a white canvas bag, and given to the setters-to in the pit, who filled the role assigned to bottle-holders in human contests. The sportsmen made their bets much as they would on a racehorse. "A guinea on the red" cries one, "Who'll take a sovereign against the grey?" cries another. It was the general custom to compete in mains, or battles, in which each owner matched a number of his own cocks against an equal number of another's. Bets were usually decided by a number of contests, but now and then a heavy wager would be laid on the issue of a single encounter.

Cock-fighting chairs are still occasionally to be seen. The sitter straddled them and had a rest to lean on; some had space for a referee's paraphernalia.

Most people, even if they didn't altogether approve of cock fighting, would perhaps still be willing to call it a sport. Cock throwing however, would disgust even the least squeamish, and it seems quite incredible that it was once considered an entertainment. Even old John Greenfield of Pet-

worth, who wrote about cock fighting with some affection, admits that cock throwing was simply a disgusting, low, barbarous practice, without a bit of science or skill to redeem it.

It was mainly practised in Sussex on Shrove Tuesday. Weighted sticks were thrown at a helpless cock, tethered by a leg. The winner was the thrower who knocked out the cock and grabbed it before it recovered. Twopence a throw was said to be the charge, and the birds must have suffered for some while before being finally knocked unconscious. It was still popular in Billingshurst late in the 18th century, many people coming miles into the village on Shrove Tuesday to take part. A brave local pastor, the Rev. William Evershed, of the Unitarian Church, wrote a 26-line poem entitled "The Cock's Remonstrance on Shrove Tuesday", and pinned it to his church door. It obviously had a good effect, because soon afterwards the cruel practice was abandoned.

A Brighton variant had the cock placed in a pot and suspended across one of the Lanes. The players had four shies with a heavy stick known as a libbet, and the cock was given to the person who broke the pot. Cock-in-the-pot, as it was known, was not exactly humane, but at least it would seem to be one step less cruel than the cock throwing.

But even in the days when cock throwing was going on, there were people who could see how cruel and degrading it was. At Lewes, from 1758 to 1780, the town crier annually gave warning not to throw at cocks on Shrove Tuesday.

A similar game, known as thrashing the hen, was also popular in Sussex. All those taking part were blindfolded and armed with sticks, except the hoodman, who carried bells and a hen in a sack. The hen went as a prize to the contestant who managed to beat it to death. I have often wondered how they ever managed to persuade anyone to take on the job of hoodman.

Top left: A badger dig at Little Thakeham, near Pulborough c.1900. Badger baiting sometimes accompanied cock fighting in the days when such things were considered good sport.
Photo: Courtesy Mr W. Truscott
Above: Cock throwing on Shrove Tuesday, as shown on an old print.
Below: Billingshurst, one of the places in Sussex where "Cock Throwing" was carried out on Shrove Tuesday.
Photo: Courtesy Mr I. Wale

Bat and Trap

Bat and Trap (or, to give it two of its other names, Trap Bat or Bat and Ball) has been played in Brighton on Good Friday for longer than anyone can remember. Just when it became associated in Brighton with Good Friday nobody knows. In most places, it is a game not associated with any particular day.

For the rules I cannot do better than quote from Ralph Merrifield's article "Good Friday Customs in Sussex" in *Sussex Archaeological Collections*:

> *The ball is placed on the lever of the shoe-shaped trap, and is made to rise by a sharp tap with the bat on the end of the lever. The batsman then tries to strike it downwards and in the direction of the fieldsmen, who stand in a line about forty to fifty feet from the trap. He is out if he fails to hit the ball after three attempts; if the ball falls short of the line of fieldsmen; or is caught by one of them; or if the man who stops the ball succeeds in hitting the end of the trap with it.*

I have heard the game described as a sort of cricket match minus a wicket. Traditionally it is always played at Brighton on The Level, a piece of open ground just north of St Peter's Church, usually between teams organized by local public houses and the Brighton and District Labour Club. At one time a barrel of beer for the players was paid for either by the losing team or by collections, but, according to a letter from a correspondent in Brighton printed in the *Daily Telegraph* in August 1979, it was at that time donated by a local brewery.

The *Daily Telegraph* letter followed a piece printed a few days earlier by Mark Temple, headed "Batswoman Takes Over", which described the game of Bat and Trap as it had been played at Canterbury for six centuries and made the point that there were at that time six women's teams in Kent. The *Daily Telegraph* correspondence also brought forth a letter from someone who remembered playing the game at school in Winchester about seventy years before.

As editor of a national magazine, I can remember getting a spirited correspondence going on the subject of the game and its origins. Readers mentioned its popularity in many parts of the country under different names and guises. Among the names mentioned were Piggy, Cattie, Peggy, and Buck an' Stick. The similarity to the ancient games of Tip-Cat and Knur-and-Spel was pointed out.

In his book *Dear Amberley*, the Rev. E. Noel Staines recalls that the sports enjoyed by the children of the village in Mr Humphrey's meadow included cricket, bat-trap, swings, and running for ginger beer. Mr W. Creighton of Hassocks remembered a game from the 1920s that he knew as Trippett, which by his description seems to be similar to Bat and Trap.

Mr C.E.J. Walkden of Rustington went back in his memory to 1910-11, when he was a small boy in Brighton and his father looked after the equipment for the game of Bat and Trap, which was used on outings by his church men's club. The club would go by train to places such as Arundel, then hire a waggonette to take them on to the Black Rabbit for a meal followed by the game. His description of the rules follows closely that given in Mr Merrifield's article.

Sid Manville, in his recollections of Brighton between the wars, *Everything seems Smaller*, remembers Good Friday Bat and Trap on The Level as a glorious romp, without many recognizable rules. If you wanted to bat you had to line up at about 9.30 a.m. in order to get a bash at 11.00 a.m.

It seems that in the past Bat and Trap was as popular in Brighton on Good Friday as were marbles and skipping. Now the tradition has lapsed and most of the Bat and Trap sets have found their way into Sussex museums.

Right: Bat-and-Trap being played on The Level at Brighton on Good Friday in the 1930s. Photo: Ralph Merrifield

Below: Bat-and-Trap set as used in Brighton on Good Friday, although the game was played at other times of the year elsewhere. Photo: Worthing Museum

Clubs and Friendly Societies

Long before the National Health Service came into being or National Insurance existed in any form, the ordinary men of Sussex (and other counties) had organized their own insurance against sickness and death by means of benefit clubs or friendly societies. There are many records of clubs in Sussex and in the West of England, although they were not unknown in the North. The history of these clubs goes back several centuries, but they became particularly active during the 19th and early 20th centuries. Working men met regularly in the village pub, getting together to alleviate the problems caused by sickness, accidents, and death at a time when there was no other form of aid available.

The annual meetings of the clubs, although open to all, were attended mainly by the regulars. What the world at large did see and enjoy were the annual "walks" or processions, which took place most often on Whit Monday. The men in their Sunday best, which in those days still meant snowy white smocks, would assemble at their pub headquarters, march to the church for a service, and then return to the pub for a feast. In some villages Club Day became the most important day of the year – a time of carnival with the whole village joining in. One little girl when asked what were the chief festivals of the church, replied, "Christmas, Easter, and Club Day".

Sometimes this annual fête became more important that the serious side of club business – so much so that I have heard that some clubs went into liquidation after spending all their money on the eating and drinking. But, normally, Club Day was an excellent way to keep the club together and to show that something good could come out of the alehouse. The men would wear smocks and, often, coloured sashes or rosettes, white gloves, and even top hats. They carried such things as banners and flags and staves, brass rods, or, more commonly, hazel wands. Folklorists find much of interest in the significance of the peeled staves often carried in these annual processions. It has been suggested that they may have originated in memory of the Canterbury pilgrim's staves. The fairly common use of beech for the staves almost certainly goes back to an old tradition, rooted perhaps in pre-Christian springtime rituals.

Some of the larger villages had more than one club, each centred on a particular pub. In 1887 the Petworth clubs united for their Club Day, and taking part were the Old Blue Friendly Society, dating from 1794; the Swan Friendly; the Masons' Arms; the Odd Fellows; the Red, White, and Blue; the Foresters; and the Junior Foresters. The Park Club (confined to those who worked for Lord Leconfield) held its Club Day separately from the others.

The best-known Sussex Club is probably Harting Old Club, which was founded very early in the 19th century and is still going strong today – possibly the only club of this sort still in existence in the county.

Mr Barton, who lived at Rushlake Green, near Heathfield, told me about the benefit club he remembered from his youth. They paraded once a year on a Tuesday in May and, carrying staves, marched in procession from the pub to the church. Anyone who became drunk on Club Day was fined half-a-crown, a large amount in those days. Mr Barton recalled one man once putting half-a-crown ready on the table in front of him, before he started drinking.

A few years ago, the Barnes Green Friendly Society disbanded, ending a piece of Sussex history that had lasted for well over a century – the benefit society activities of the club had ceased, though, just before World War II. The oldest member, who had joined the club in 1902, received his share of the money in hand, along with about thirty others. In the early days the membership was around one hundred, each man paying a regular small donation and receiving benefits to a maximum of £5 when necessary.

Like other village clubs, the Barnes Green Society knew how to enjoy its annual Club Day. As one member recalled, it was a "right binge!" The procession of members, headed by a band, set off from the *Queen's Head* at 9.30 a.m. for a service at Itchingfield church, halting along the way for beer and refreshments. After the service, and coffee in the rectory, they marched on to Muntham House for lunch in a big marquee. One rector, it seems, complained about the use of the churchyard by club members, so the church-service arrangements were changed. The local pub held a Cherry Fair on the night before Club Day and when the procession was over on the day there was a village fair.

The oldest of the Sussex clubs would appear to be the Chailey Friendly Society, which was instituted in 1782. The society's motto was "Love the Brotherhood – Fear God – Honour the King". There was an entry fee and a subscription and the club's finances were augmented by fines imposed on members who infringed the rules. The annual Club Day was 4 June, when the members assembled at 10.00 a.m. and, after a roll call, proceeded in procession to the church for a service. The feast that followed was paid for out of club funds – an amount not exceeding two shillings for each member was allocated for it.

In spite of occasional lapses and excesses, the village clubs were of great value, and the men who carried the considerable burden of keeping the accounts and generally managing the club's affairs, are to be greatly commended – particularly when we consider that in many cases their education must have been of a fairly meagre kind.

Above: The annual Club Walk at Northam in East Sussex about 1900. The men's white smocks and peeled wands, are well in evidence. *Photo: Mrs Perigoe*

Below: An undated photograph of the annual Club Day at South Harting. Outside the White Hart are members and friends of the Harting Old Club, which has been in existence since early in the 19th century. *Photo: Mr R. Merryfield*

Eccentrics and Worthies

Horsham has always had its fair share of characters, personalities, or eccentrics – unusual and fascinating people whatever we care to call them.

Miss Elizabeth Gatford died in Horsham in 1799, leaving a reputation for strange, almost hermit-like behaviour. For twenty years before her death she had not left her mansion, allowing her coach to fall to pieces and her horses to graze undisturbed in the fields. Her will directed that her body be deposited in a stone coffin lined with lead, and that it should remain uninterred for a month, during which time it was to be bathed in spirits of wine every night, at a cost of £20. The funeral took place at night (not entirely unusual at that time) and the body was contained within four coffins, the outer one of marble. Miss Gatford was borne to her final resting place, a vault in the Dissenting Meeting House ground, by 18 farmers. She left £15 annually to her cats, dogs, and other animals – not, apparently, including her horses. She also left five guineas annually to be spent on bread for the poor.

Howard Dudley, who was born in 1821, seems a much happier character. He lived with his Quaker family, in London for the first few years of his life, but, while still a boy, moved with his mother and sister to Easebourne, near Midhurst. Here he became keenly interested in history and archaeology. When he was only 14, he wrote a book entitled *Juvenile Researches, or a Description of some of the Principle Towns in the Western Part of Sussex and the Borders of Hampshire*. This he alone researched, illustrated, and set up in type; he alone prepared the printing blocks for 45 of his own drawings; he alone produced the book, page by page, on his own small printing press. A second edition followed a year later, with additional text, and this time 70 drawings. The last item in the book was a poem entitled "An Address to Horsham".

It must have been about this time that the family moved to Albion Terrace in Horsham, because his next book (published in 1836 when he was still only 15), was *History and Antiquities of Horsham*. This predated Lady Hurst's book of a similar title by some thirty years. Again it was illustrated with his own engravings. The printer's imprint on the final page was "Howard Dudley, Millbank Street".

In 1845, at the age of 25, Dudley became a professional wood engraver, moved to Edinburgh, and married. He died at the early age of 44 in 1864, in London, before he could proceed with an intended *History of Midhurst*. Although he was not strictly speaking a Horsham, or even a Sussex, man, he had a great affection for the county. In 1865 the *Gentleman's Magazine* printed a pleasant memorial to this talented man, calling him "a person of gentlemanly manners and a delightful companion".

Our next Horsham character was neither well-to-do, nor well educated; he lived and died without any kind of memorial, and I am not even sure of his dates, although he must have been around during the latter part of the 19th century. His name was Dick Fillary, although many townsfolk knew him simply as "Ole Dick". I suspect that he was not as daft as some people believed – perhaps he was just an easy-going chap who liked to make people laugh. There are a lot of good stories about him. When he was to meet a man at the Fox and Hounds public house, he made an arrangement – "If you get there first, you put a stone of the wall. If I get there first, I'll knock it off". Another time he was helping a local farmer, and he asked, "Have you counted those sheep yet?" "Yep, I counted 'em, all except one, and 'ee run about so much, I couldn't count of 'ee". Another day he was seen walking

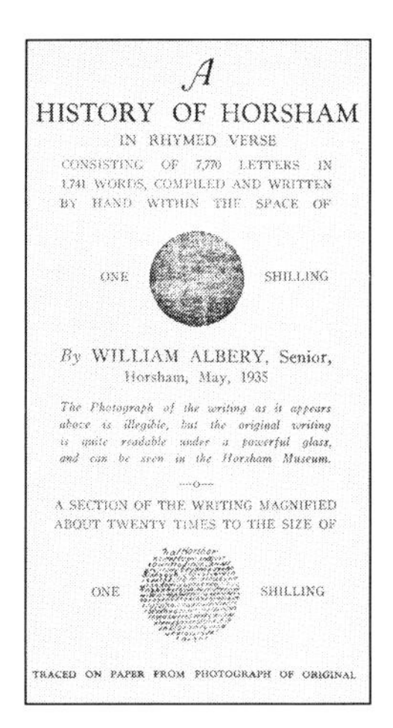
A

HISTORY OF HORSHAM

IN RHYMED VERSE

CONSISTING OF 7,770 LETTERS IN 1,741 WORDS, COMPILED AND WRITTEN BY HAND WITHIN THE SPACE OF

ONE SHILLING

By WILLIAM ALBERY, Senior, Horsham, May, 1935

The Photograph of the writing as it appears above is illegible, but the original writing is quite readable under a powerful glass, and can be seen in the Horsham Museum.

—o—

A SECTION OF THE WRITING MAGNIFIED ABOUT TWENTY TIMES TO THE SIZE OF

ONE SHILLING

TRACED ON PAPER FROM PHOTOGRAPH OF ORIGINAL

Top left: An example of the fine Caligraphy of Horsham's William Albery, who was well-known as a local historian. This is from his rhymed history of the town, published as a booklet in 1943, and originally written by hand within the space of one shilling.

Some Horsham Characters

down Middle Street with a look of fierce determination on his face, and with his hands held out firmly in front of him. When asked the reason, he replied "Can't stop now, been sent to measure a door". When a friend of his was given the job of cleaning the pigs out, a task that carried extra pay, Dick was heard to remark "T'aint fair – I can do all the dirty work, and Joe can clean the pigs out". Evidently Joe got paid more than Dick at other times, because on another occasion he was heard to complain, "There's ole Joe, gets eighteenpence a day for night work, and I get nothin' – that's somethin', aint it?"

Our final personality should really have a whole article, or even a whole book written about him. One of Horsham's best-known sons, Henry Burstow was born on 11 December 1826 in the Bishopric, next to the *Jolly Ploughboy*. One of a family of nine children, his father was a clay-pipe maker – a popular occupation at that time. He attended a dame school in the Bishopric, helping at Albery's, the harness makers in West Street, in his free time – for sixpence a day.

He knew well over four hundred songs, learning them easily from his family and other local singers as well as from ballad sheets, which were sold in the streets and outside the pubs for a few pence. He had a marvellous memory, both for his songs and for events that had taken place during his own life and the lifetime of his parents and grandparents. Many of the famed folk-song experts of the day collected songs from him, including Lucy Broadwood and Ralph Vaughan Williams. He would walk out to Rusper to sing to Miss Broadwood whenever she invited him. Vaughan Williams used a cylinder phonograph to record his singers, later transcribing the songs at his leisure. It is rumoured that some of the wax cylinders of Henry's singing still exist, but so far I have been unsuccessful in tracking them down.

In 1911 a book of his recollections, *Reminiscences of Horsham* was published locally; it was ghosted by a young historian, William Albery. A second edition appeared the following year. It is now extremely valuable as a record of Horsham life as it was in the late 19th and very early 20th centuries, seen from the viewpoint of an ordinary working man. Among the many events remembered in the book are an earthquake in 1833, a violent storm in 1836, the coronation of Queen Victoria in 1838, and the last public hanging in Horsham (with some 3,000 people present) in 1844. Henry Burstow died in 1916, aged 90, poor in material things (he only narrowly escaped the workhouse) but rich in many other ways.

Below: A familiar sight in Horsham's streets in the 1960s – "Yorkey's" barrow, used to fetch coke from the local gas works.
Photo: Mr F. Holmes

Old Pub Games

The Sussex countryman of the past spent much of his brief leisure, and his even more limited spare cash, in the village inn. It was largely a man's world, and although his wife undoubtedly regretted the loss of the pennies that passed into the publican's pockets, there was not a lot she could do about it. A man had to have some form of recreation and, after all, women had their housework, their needlework, and the children.

Drink was absurdly cheap by present-day standards, although when a farm labourer earned well under a pound a week to keep a family it may not have seemed so to him. Mr Barton from Rushlake Green, near Heathfield, told me of the night when his older brother broke his clay pipe. He called at the local pub at 9.00 p.m. on his way home and for sixpence was able to buy a pint of beer (twopence), five Woodbine cigarettes (twopence), a pipe (halfpenny), and a box of matches (a farthing), and still end up with a penny-farthing change.

There was much public drunkenness, and the sight of drunks in the street was not considered a matter for undue comment. But it must not be concluded that every working man was a drunkard. Many drank in moderation on all but very special occasions, and others were total abstainers – in fact the teetotal movement was a very active force in Victorian life. But many men took pride in their capacity to hold their drink. One man told me that on one occasion he bet that he could drink the same number of pints of beer as he scored runs in the day's cricket match. He scored 22, and duly downed that number of pints in the pub after the match; then he walked home.

Village pubs offered a good deal besides drink. There was the companionship, the warmth, and the entertainment – games such as ring-the-bull, toad-in-the-hole, and shove-ha'penny.

Ring-the-bull, or ringing-the-bull, was not too difficult once you got the knack. Rules were almost non-existent; all you had to do was to get the ring over the hook more times than your opponent. The hook could be a plain hook or it might be a stuffed head with a hook on the end of the nose. The ring was of brass, fixed to a six-foot cord, in front of and about four feet away from the hook. You held the ring in your right hand, and swung it on to the hook.

The ring had to travel in a curve in order to strike the hook at an angle and different players had their own particular techniques. Bob Copper, in his book *Early to Rise*, speaks of a man who would turn his back on the bull, and send the ring sailing up towards the grandfather clock in the corner, yet somehow it would swing round and usually end up in the desired place. Three successful shots in succession were supposed to win a free pot of beer, but this rule may not have always been honoured because some players could ring the bull time after time with unerring accuracy. Sometimes the stuffed head would receive such punishment from the players, that it would cease to resemble the original animal.

Ring-the-bull is now a rare pub game, although there are a few pubs in Sussex where the equipment can still be seen. A less-complicated version is a simple board covered with numbered hooks at which rubber rings are thrown.

Another old pub game was toad-in-the-hole, which existed in two distinct versions, one much more complex than the other. The most interesting might be considered the forerunner of the modern pin-table. It was about the size of a tea trolley, with the flat top having a number of holes, a miniature

Left: A simple Toad-in-the-Hole, discovered quite by chance being used on a sideshow at a Sussex fête.

Ring-the-Bull and Toad-in-the-Hole

wheel, and a model toad. Metal discs had to be pitched into the numbered holes, or the toad's mouth, which presumably was the equivalent of a bull's-eye.

The other type of toad-in-the-hole consisted of a lead-covered box standing about twenty-one inches from the floor. In the centre was a single round hole about two inches in diameter, and the object of the game was to flip a metal disc or coin into this hole. Points were awarded for the number of times the disc entered the hole. I was told that the game was played originally with George III twopenny pieces, which weighed exactly two ounces. As these disappeared, because people liked to use them as two-ounce weights, so metal discs had to be substituted. Sometimes the discs provided by a pub bore the name of the house stamped on it. The lead around the centre hole in the toad would in time become pitted with dents, and an expert player could make use of these when pitching.

There is a beautiful toad-in-the-hole game in Horsham Museum, and there are also a few still around in pubs in East Sussex.

While I was searching for information on bulls and toads, I came across a toad being used in a side-show at a summer fête. The group of young men looking after it must have been puzzled by my excited recognition. It consisted of a wooden box with a round hole in the centre, and customers were having far more trouble pitching metal discs into the hole than they expected. There should have been a bell to ring whenever the discs found their way through the hole, but sadly this was no longer operating. The discs were removed through a drawer at the front of the box. I was told that the toad had been discovered rotting away in a Worthing attic, and the finder was not sure exactly what he had found, until it was recognized by a friend who had seen one in use in a Lewes pub. Since then it had been in regular use in a Worthing club, and had been borrowed for the day of the fête.

Above: A splendid Toad-in-the-Hole game, now owned by Horsham Museum. *Photo: Horsham Museum*

More Pub Games

Shove ha'penny was once a very popular pub game, although nowadays it would probably be considered very tame. It has an aristocratic pedigree, as its devotees claim that it originated with the shovel-board of Elizabethan times. Some of the shove-ha'penny boards were very large, just as shovel-boards were. There is one in Horsham Museum; that, although large, may be only half of the original table. It came to the museum from Horsham Park House and was given by the Hurst family. When last used in its original home, it was in the kitchen, to which it must have been moved from one of the grander rooms, perhaps with the advent of more fashionable furniture in the 18th century.

Most shove-ha'penny boards however (and there are still a few about) are much smaller than this; about the size of a bagatelle board. The game is played with brass discs, the size of an old half-penny; although it has been played with larger discs (when presumably the alternative name of shove-penny applied).

The boards are usually made of finely polished hardwood, as was the one I remember from my own childhood. There are also boards made of slate or marble. Lines across the board divide it into nine beds, with two lines parallel to the length of the board marking the boundaries of the playing area. Scores are chalked on the spaces made by these lines and the edge of the board. Five "ha'pennies" are used, and two people or two teams of two may play. The players put the discs slightly over the edge of the front of the board, and strike them with the palm of the hand. When all five discs have been played, each disc within two of the horizontal lines is scored; each bed may contain a score of three, but any further score in that bed counts to one's opponent. The score of three in one bed is known as a full house.

If there is doubt about whether a disc is within the bed (and there often is), then another disc is run along the line to see if it makes the doubtful one move. Some very well-made boards have a movable brass strip inset instead of a line, and this can be moved gently upwards to provide a positive test.

Shove-ha'penny boards are not confined to pubs, but may be found in private houses, sometimes relegated to the attic, but occasionally still in regular use.

A few Sussex inns still have a spinning jenny mounted on the ceiling of the bar. This is a large revolving pointer, or dial, which can be set spinning by the publican or one of the customers. There seem to be several possible reasons for such an intriguing piece of equipment, and perhaps more than one applied at different times. One use to which it was put was to decide who should pay for a round of drinks; sometimes this was known as twizzling. Bob Copper says that sometimes the points were marked with numbers, or with the letters M.Y.M.Y. (M = Me, Y = You). Rhoda Leigh, writing in 1930, speaks of it as being rather like roulette, but comments that darts were rapidly supplanting it in popularity at that time.

The most fascinating reason advanced for the existence of a spinning jenny in a bar parlour, is that it was once used by smugglers to divide their spoils. As we know that smuggling was very widespread in Sussex, and that many smugglers operated with the ready connivance of innkeepers, this seems perfectly feasible. Peter and Jan Bench of Burpham's *George and Dragon* had no doubt that their spinning jenny was used by smugglers to "divvy" up their spoils. The inn is sited right beside Burpham Camp,

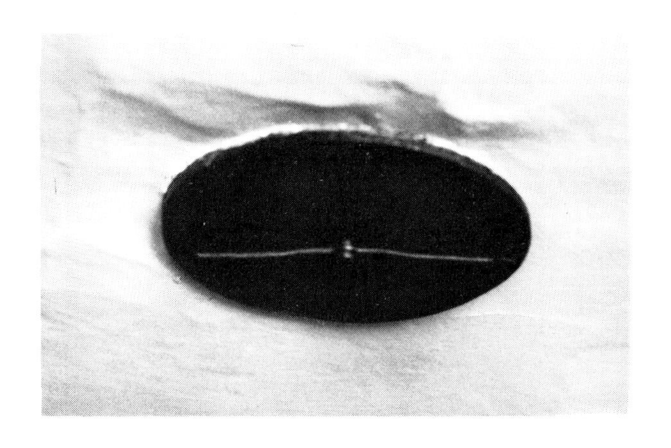

Left: The Spinning Jenny on the ceiling of the George and Dragon at Burpham. Once used by smugglers to divide their spoils, most of the diners who eat in the restaurant beneath it, are probably quite unaware it is there.

Shoving, Spinning, and Skittling

and on the far side of the camp is Jacob's Ladder of seventy steps, which it was said was used by the smugglers to bring their brandy and silks from the river to the pub. Burpham's spinning jenny is on the ceiling of what is now the restaurant of the *George and Dragon*, and I was pleased to find that it is still in good working order.

Ursula Ayling of the *Spotted Cow*, Angmering, told me that the spinning jenny in her inn was undoubtedly used by smugglers for dividing their gains. The inn has a legend about a woman smuggler, Norma, who was the cause of many men's deaths. She is said to walk the premises, to make glasses leap from the shelves, and to mystify customers with strange smells. As far as I know she has not laid hands on the spinning jenny.

Another popular pub game in Sussex, which has survived in modern forms, is skittles. Several versions existed, both indoors and out. Inside, the pins might be arranged in a circle, with a larger pin, the queen, in the centre. These were the targets for a large ball called a cheese. Another variant had the skittles themselves shaped like big fat cheeses. The balls were thrown, not rolled, and, as with all these games, experts could do wonderful things with them. Another name for skittles with wooden balls was "corners".

When the skittle alley was outdoors it might be in the inn yard, or even a separate entity. A related game was described by Marcus Woodward, writing in 1938. In this, a heavy coin or token (possibly one used for toad-in-the-hole) was thrown across the room at a cork set on a table. The cork had a farthing on top and the object was to dislodge the coin so that it fell beyond a circle drawn round the cork.

A game once played in Sussex pubs and elsewhere, was Up Jenkins. It also had several alternative names, such as tippet and spoof. There were several variations of the game, but this is how Mr R.H. Charters of Wadhurst described it to me. Two teams sat on either side of a table, one side having sixpence hidden in one person's hand. The other team had a captain, who gave the orders. If anyone obeyed an order from any player other than the captain, then the sixpence was forfeited. The first order was "Up Jenkins", and the hands came up with clenched fists. Then followed "Elephant Gate Openers" (opening and shutting hands very quickly), "Creepy Crawlies" (scrabbling about on the table), "Butterflies" (waving the hands up and down), "Lobster Pots" (fingers down and dancing on the table). The climax was "Smashoms", when all the hands came down with a crash on the table. The point of all this was to discover who had the sixpence. The captain finally ordered all the hands to be withdrawn from the table except the one he had decided was holding the coin. If he was right, then the team with the sixpence handed it over to the other side; if not they kept it for another turn. I have been told that this was a game reserved for Sundays in some pubs, when other games were considered unsuitable.

The Tipteerers

Around Christmas, and particularly on Boxing Day, the Christmas mummers (in Sussex they were called "tipteerers", or "tipteers") visited the big houses and the pubs with their ancient death-and-resurrection play. The actors, always male in the past, played the same characters year after year, until death or ill health brought someone else into the cast. The players numbered anything from four to six or even more, and the parts they played – King George (or sometimes Saint George), the Turkish Knight, Beelzebub (the Devil), the Doctor, Little Johnny Jack, and Father Christmas (the compere) remained the same – although sometimes topical heroes such as Nelson or Napoleon were introduced.

The texts also remained the same, but were subject to minor variations through the years – they were seldom committed to paper and the words, like those of folk songs, might be changed because of faulty memory or to take account of current happenings.

The costumes were basic, often merely old clothes with bright pieces of material sewn all over them (surprisingly effective), or sometimes the characters would dress in clothes roughly approximating the parts they were playing. Sometimes faces would be blackened – this was probably always the case in earlier times. It was considered fitting that the audience should not recognize those taking part – even if everyone really knew exactly who was in the play each year. By the 19th century this practice seems to have largely died out.

In retrospect it is easy to see old traditions such as the tipteerers' plays, continuing in an unbroken thread through the years. In fact there were almost certainly years when the thread was broken for varying reasons, to be resumed again after a lapse of perhaps several years. The history of most folk customs would, I suspect, be found invariably to consist of breaks and revivals if it were possible to chart them with absolute accuracy. None of our Sussex plays survived by traditional means into modern times, although there have been many revivals since about the 1920s, many based firmly on older folk's memories.

This is how George Attrill of Fittleworth, opened the play "King George and the Dragon":

In Comes I, Old Father Christmas,
Am I welcome, or am I not?
I'm sometimes cold and sometimes hot,
but I hope old Father Christmas will never be forgot.
Ladies and Gentlemen, I am here but a short time to stay,
But I will give you a little pleasure,
To pass the time, before I go away.

George played Father Christmas, and did not need a false beard for the part. He acted as compere of the play, and his opening speech was typical of a great many of the Sussex plays.

The origins of the plays have been lost, but the gist is in the old story "The Seven Champions of Christendon". Allusions in the plays to the Turkish Knight have been linked to the Crusades, but we do not know if this character has been grafted on to a much older story.

The Boxgrove Tipteers flourished in the 1930s, using a play that was a combination of texts from East Preston and Iping. It was in 1911 that Mr Foard, a farm worker, revived the East Preston play, having taken part in it as a boy. World War I put an end to this revival (as it did to so many other folk customs), but in 1927 the Boxgrove Tipteers came into being, due to the enthusiasm of Mr R.J. Sharp, who had played fiddle for the East Preston gang.

Left: The Rusper Mummers Play performed at the Royal Oak, Langhurst Wood, near Horsham in 1984.
Photo: Broadwood Morris Men

Christmas Plays and Mummers

The Iping version of the play came from Mr Frank Dawtrey, a cowman, who also contributed several Sussex songs and two dances ("The Bonny Breast-knot" and "Over the Sticks").

The Boxgrove men continued to present their play and sing their songs, including "The Moon Shone Bright" and "Sweet Rosy Morn", right up to the outbreak of World War II. In 1937 they took part in the English Folk Dance and Song Society's Festival at the Royal Albert Hall.

Since that time there have been many more revivals, often by morris men and folk-song clubs. The Chanctonbury Ring Morris Men perform the Steyning play on Boxing Day and New Year's Day. The Broadwood Morris Men present a play based on that collected by Lucy Broadwood of Lyne House, Rusper, from local tipteerers in 1880 and 1881. She wrote: "They clustered together, wooden swords in hand, at the close of their play 'St George and the Turk' and sang, wholly unconscious of the contrast between the solemnity of the carol, and the grotesqueness of their appearance; for they wore dresses of coloured calico, heavily trimmed with shreds of ribbon, gaudy paper fringes and odd ornaments."

After 1881 the play ceased to be performed in the Horsham area until Christmas 1971, when the Broadwood Men, having obtained the text of the play from the folklorist Margaret Dean-Smith, enacted it once again. Additional characters have since been added and, as in the past, the play as it is performed each year is extended or varied as seems appropriate.

Most mummers conclude their play with a song or carol, sometimes one having no connection with the text of the play or with the season. The Broadwood Men conclude their play with the Sussex Mummer's Carol, as noted by Lucy Broadwood:

O mortal men, remember well, when Christ our Lord was born,
He was crucified betwixt two thieves and crowned with the thorn,
And crowned with the thorn.

She published the carol in her *English Traditional Songs and Carols* in 1908, having obtained the words and melody through a competition for old songs in the *West Sussex Gazette* in 1905. She notes that it was sung in about 1878-81 by mummers from the neighbourhood of Horsham.

In dealing with old customs such as tipteering plays, one must always be careful not to over-romanticize. Like the Christmas carollers, the wassailers, and the bonfire boys, the end product of the whole operation was the supply of much-needed coppers from the pockets of the audience. The tipteerers went where there was money to be had, namely the big houses and the drinking places. Their visit was expected and looked upon as part of the Christmas scene, and gifts in kind and in coin were offered and accepted with dignity. Their visit to the big houses was probably one of several made during the Christmas season by various village groups, including the carollers, the local band, and perhaps the hand-bell ringers.

Right: The Broadwood Morris Men perform the local Mummers Play each Boxing Day in Horsham's Carfax.

Bonfire Night

Guy Fawkes Night, 5 November, is the night of the year when Sussex people really let themselves go. Otherwise law-abiding citizens throw discretion to the wind, dressing up in outlandish costumes and parading the streets; even the present-day trend towards religious ecumenism is forgotten for 24 hours.

Why Sussex should care so much for its bonfires is not entirely clear. It has been suggested that Lewes, the otherwise peaceful East Sussex town that lifts its skirts on this one night of the year, has particular memories to keep its anti-Guy Fawkes fervour alive, for 17 Protestant martyrs gave their lives here. But Lewes is by no means the only Sussex town that celebrates bonfire night with particular abandon. It seems that East Sussex has slightly more enthusiasm than West, but this may be argued. Towns with particular bonfire-night traditions include Battle, Billingshurst, Hastings, Littlehampton, Rotherfield, and Rye, but most villages and towns celebrated it in some degree in the past.

No doubt Lewes had its bonfires long before the gunpowder plot of 1605, but it is on record that the year following the abortive plot Lewes folk celebrated the non-event with a bonfire on Cliffe Hill. The custom of dragging flaming tar barrels along the streets soon became part of the Lewes celebrations, as did the street processions. It is said that a famous Southover character, Old Betty, could be found each bonfire night dragging a blazing tar barrel and smoking her pipe.

In the early part of the 19th century, the scenes enacted in Lewes on 5 November each year were completely wild and uncontrolled. Year by year there was trouble, leading to arrests and subsequent prison sentences. In 1847 large numbers of extra police were brought in, including a contingent from London and no less than 170 Specials. For some years following there were wild scenes each November, and the local newspaper, *The Sussex Advertiser*, thundered more loudly, calling for an end to the celebrations. Eventually, more organized Bonfire Societies began to emerge, and Lewes was no longer a town to be avoided at all costs on 5 November. Yet it would be foolish to suppose that it is ever a place for the faint-hearted on that night. As George Townsend of Lewes told me, on Guy Fawkes Night you never wear anything but your oldest clothes and you set out expecting the worst, wearing if possible a pair of goggles. In 1904 the firework named after the town, the Lewes Rouser, was banned, and in 1905 the custom of dragging fiery tar barrels through the streets came to an end – now they are merely thrown into the river. But some shops still find it advisable to board up their windows, and a certain amount of rowdyism inevitably takes place.

Lewes was not the only place where the activities of the bonfire boys was frowned upon. The *West Sussex Gazette* of 12 November 1863 carried an impassioned letter from a reader about the ordeal of residents of a country house close to the South Downs. On 5 November the occupants were visited at 8.00 a.m. by seven small boys with paper caps on their heads, brandishing cow horns. After reciting their bonfire hymn, they blew a flourish on their horns and then had to be driven away by force. An hour later came three bigger boys dressed in the same manner but with blackened faces. They had with them a guy, which they planted before the front door, invoking curses upon it. This sort of thing continued throughout the morning and, after a lull in the afternoon, was taken up again in the evening. The correspondent ended with the pious

Left: An oil painting by an unknown artist of Lewes bonfire c.1876. A burning effigy of the Pope can be seen.

"Please to Remember..."

hope that the "plough boys and yokels" might soon learn that nearly all England has given up such mummery. Evidently, Sussex was maintaining its traditions longer than elsewhere, as it often has done.

Many of our bonfire-night celebrations are based on little more than a desire to break loose from the bounds of convention on at least one night of the year. Not all damage is caused by fireworks or fire; sometimes the celebrations are used as an excuse for vandalism. The search for burnable materials can also cause trouble. Helena Hall of Lindfield told the story of the elderly man who urged boys to "pile 'em on" as heavy bundles of faggots were thrown on to the flames. Not until the next day did he discover that the faggots were his own, brought round from the back of the house while he cheered the boys on from the front. When the town's tollgates were removed in 1884, both gates were burnt in a big bonfire on 5 November, while on another occasion Miss Hall's own gate was ripped from its hinges and her fence torn up to help swell one of the fires in the High Street.

At Rye, bonfire night was considered a proper time for practical jokes. Once revellers put a man up to his neck in a tar barrel. Barrels filled with burning tar were rolled down Conduit Hill, and shopkeepers boarded up their shop fronts as the town prepared for a state of siege.

Mr H.R. Goatcher of Washington told me of a bonfire night he remembered from his childhood in East Preston. The one local policeman had been called to Littlehampton and, with the village left unguarded, the local lads decided to roll tar barrels up the road to start a bonfire in front of Preston Cottage. At the crossroads they gathered all the burnable material they could find, including pea and bean sticks from the local allotments (the policeman's included). One lady brought out a cradle, saying she would have no further use for it. The result was a tremendous fire that was still burning so strongly the next morning that the carters had difficulty in getting their horses round the corner on their way to work.

At Hastings Museum they have the banner of the Hastings Bonfire Society, dating from the time when the Hastings celebrations vied in size and scale with those of Lewes and Battle. The banner is of painted canvas, 8ft x 12ft. The museum also has a guy's head that belonged to the Bohemia Bonfire Boys, one of the local societies. Apparently the guys' heads were too valuable to be burnt – they were taken off the effigies each year at the last moment and retained for future use.

In the 1800s the Horsham bonfire-night celebrations were some of the best in the county. The size and extent varied through the years, but there were always bonfires in some form, with sometimes as many as three – the largest always being in the Carfax where the heat scorched the paint off some of the houses. In 1870 the Horsham Bonfire Boys Society was formed, and huge guys, 10ft or 12ft high, were paraded round the town with bands, trees of fire, and performers in carts, on horseback, and on foot.

Right: Crawley High Street in November 1914 and the last 5th of November bonfire to be built in the roadway. It was decided that the disruption to traffic, and the damage to the road surface could no longer be tolerated. *Photo: Mr T.J. Laker*

Beating the Bounds

Rogation-time (the days immediately preceding Ascension Day) was traditionally the period when groups of Sussex villagers would perambulate the bounds of their parish, stopping at key points to impress the boundaries on the younger members of the community. This was done in several different ways, by beating the ground with rods or bunches of twigs or, sometimes, by beating or bumping the boys themselves. This was very much a church custom, with the local vicar and church officials in attendance. No doubt the beating was done in a light-hearted manner, but the lesson was there to be learnt – parish perambulations in Rogation Week in the Diocese of Chichester were described in 1637 as for the "knowing and distinguishing the bounds of the parishes, and for obtaining God's blessing upon the fruites of the ground".

In some parishes the beating of the bounds was a well-patronized local event, with food and drink provided at certain recognized stopping places, in others it was a custom dutifully carried on by just a faithful few.

We have an account of the beating of the bounds in the parish of Burpham in 1810. On Tuesday of Rogation Week, the minister, church-wardens, and other inhabitants met at the church and from there began their procession around the bounds of the parish. At several stopping places the minister said prayers, a cross was made on the ground, and refreshments were taken. Although children were included, there is no mention of any actual beating or bumping. We do not know how many people took part – it could not have been very many because it was only a small village – but the food and drink provided included 23 gallons of ale, a very large amount of bread and cake, and an unknown quantity of cheese.

In 1950 Chiddingfold (near the Surrey-Sussex border) lost a link with the past with the death of its oldest inhabitant, who had been present at the village beating of the bounds in 1869. At this date it took two days to complete, and involved a walk of 40 miles. Even then the ceremony must have been in decline, for only three people took part.

Many places have revived their ancient bound-treading ceremonies in recent years. Old customs that have fallen into disuse are revived from time to time throughout history and few traditions continue year after year without occasional breaks. At Barcombe just 19 people participated in the bound-beating in 1802. The rite then seems to have lapsed, but it was revived in 1914, when the proceedings, which lasted two days, attracted 42 people. The ceremonies appear to have been taken very seriously. An attempt was made to keep to the line of the parish boundaries, even when this meant climbing roofs, walking through private houses, and even swimming a pond. A letter "B" was carved on a suitable oak tree, and a rather strange local tradition was observed at Bell Hole Brook, where bells were hurled into the water. The boys were bumped at several places, and so was the Barcombe parish clerk. No one seems to have minded, though, for the numbers attending increased to 53 on the second day. The late Garth Christain, writing about the 1914 revival in 1953, said that at that time there were men in Barcombe who could tell you where the village ended simply because they could still remember being bumped on the hard wealden clay 38 years before.

There are many modern revivals. One of the best known is at Chailey, where the tradition goes back to at least 1691, and where now the bounds are marked by cross-country runners, horses and riders, cyclists, and canoeists. This has developed into a challenge to other villages, with some strong competition.

The photographs shown are from Hastings around the 1920s, and here the ceremony has been observed in even more modern times during the Old Town Week celebrations. Organized by the Old Hastings Preservation Society, it takes the form of a procession of parishioners from St Clements and All Saints churches, ending in prayers before a wayside cross.

Littlehampton is another Sussex town that has revived its bound-beating. Previously, the beating had last been carried out in 1840, and there is said to be a reference to it dated 1741. The boys are up-ended and bumped on the ground and participants are given willow sticks to beat the ground. Yet another Sussex place that has practised the old ceremonies in modern times is Southwick, where the organizers are the Southwick Society. No doubt there are many other places in Sussex where this useful custom is going strong.

A relatively modern custom with a similarity to beating the bounds used to take place each Ascension Day at East Grinstead, where early in the morning the vicar, with attendant choir boys, would ceremoniously bless the market.

Top and above: Beating the Bounds at Hastings.

The Harvest Home

The final gathering in of the harvest was a very important time for the farmer and all who worked for him. The occasion was marked in different ways in different places, according to local custom, but the last load from the fields was often brought in with due solemnity, horses were often decorated (after being given extra feed), and the children of the farm workers would ride in state on their broad backs. In some places, on the last day of the harvest all the workers employed on the farm would gather in a ring and chant:

We've ploughed, we've sowed, we've reaped, we've mowed,
We've carried the last load, and never overthrowed,
Hip, Hip, Hurrah!

This ceremony was known as Hollerin' Pot. Most farms followed any celebration in the fields with a more organized feast or supper, often on the Saturday evening (presumably so that the men had the lighter duties of Sunday to help them get over the effects of the feast before they returned for normal work on Monday). The harvest supper was usually held in the largest barn on the farm, although on one estate I was told the only building big enough was a very large greenhouse. Sometimes the supper would be preceded by games, and music would be provided by the village brass band.

Occasionally, a harvest supper for a whole community would be provided, with the farmers and landowners all contributing. It would take place in the largest building available in the village. Farmers and squires were mostly happy enough to provide this annual treat for their work people, but not everyone was generous. A squire of one Sussex village (which shall remain nameless) used to give what he called a harvest home. This consisted of two buns for the village children, plus a drink of tea – but they had to take their own mugs. The adults didn't rate anything, not even a bun!

Drink usually flowed freely at harvest suppers. At the supper held in the greenhouse it was dispensed from big enamel watering cans. At South Harting, the farmer would lay down clean straw outside the barn in which the supper was held, so that the feasters, as they became too drunk to continue, could be taken out by their less-inebriated friends, and laid out on the straw until they had recovered sufficiently to resume drinking.

But some proceedings were rather more respectable – the 1863 harvest home at West Hoathly, for instance. The day began at 8.00 a.m. with the church bells ringing. The main street was decorated with flags and greenery, and at 1.30 p.m. a service was held in the church. This was followed by a procession led by the village band; farmers had provided wagons and there were such things in the parade as a huge loaf of bread carried on a wooden tray. The landowners had contributed two shillings each to pay for a feast, which was held in a marquee in Cross Field. The meal included quantities of beef, potatoes, suet pudding, plum cake, and gingerbread. The wives and children had a separate tent, in which they had a lighter meal of tea and cakes. Afterwards, those celebrants who were still in a fit state were invited to take part in sports, with various prizes.

In that same year of 1863 a harvest supper was held under canvas at Warnham Court Park. It followed a cricket match between the servants of the big house and the farm workers (the Warnham Court team won). About seventy sat down to deal with the roast beef and plum pudding under the eye of the host, Sir J.H. Pelly. Lady Pelly, meanwhile, did the honours for the wives and children in a

"We've reaped, we've mowed..."

separate tent, with the usual tea and cakes. Apparently only the men were expected to have the kind of appetite to deal with meat and vegetables.

Sometimes the harvest feast would be very formal, as at Shillinglee Park, Northchapel, in 1861. Here the celebration was attended by the Earl and Countess Winterton, Lady and Viscount Turnour, and the Rev. S. Fairles. After the supper, toys were distributed to the children, and this was followed by sports, in which, it was noted by the *West Sussex Gazette*, "Lord Turnour and the Rev. Mr Fairles took a prominent part". The *Gazette* also remarked, "These occasions tend to enhance a proper feeling in the heart of both the employer and employed."

An important part of the more informal harvest suppers was the period set apart for songs, which always followed the food. Many old favourites would be trotted out each year, with often one man being called upon for the same song year after year. For instance, there was "Bango", now known as a children's song:

The Miller's old dog lay on the mill floor,
And Bango was his name, O.
B - A - and N - G - O,
And Bango was his name, O.

The custom was for the leader to sing the two opening lines, turning to his righthand neighbour for the "B". The next man along was expected to shout "A", the "N", and so on. If a man missed his cue, then his forfeit was to drink an extra mug of ale.

Another song game was "Turning the Cup Over". This involved a mug of beer and a hat (they all wore hats in the 19th century). If the player failed to carry out the operation correctly, the mug was refilled and the drinker went through the elaborate rigmarole once more. Everyone took a turn (at wearing the hat) so the whole thing must have taken a very long time.

Toasts were an important ingredient of a successful harvest supper. A shy farm boy called upon unexpectedly to propose a toast could always fall back on this well known example of rustic wit:

Scorched bread, well buttered,
If that ain't toast, then I'm buggered.

One old man told me with great relish "when everyone was sat down, a new pipe was provided by his plate, and a pouch of tobacco sent round for each to have his fill".

And thus we must leave the Sussex farm labourers of the past, with their bellies filled with roast beef, their mugs full of beer, and their clay pipes full of tobacco. No doubt they worked all the harder the following week.

This was the scene at the Salvation Army Hall in Portslade in 1917.

Long Rope Day

As the men played marbles on Good Friday, so in many Sussex towns and villages the women skipped – other names for Good Friday (when it was not called Marbles Day) were Long Rope Day and Long Line Day. The custom seems to have been particularly prevalent during the 19th century at places along the coast. At Brighton, where the old fishing families tended to keep up time- honoured customs longer than elsewhere, it was popular until the beginning of World War II. Its venues were the fish-market Hard and streets like Ship Street, Duke Street, Middle Street, and Brighton Place.

An account in an old copy of *John O'London's Weekly* describes how two stalwart fishermen stand and turn a heavy rope while young men and women run in and out, sometimes as many as six or seven at a time. An old fisherman, who believed that the rope was used as a sign of Judas hanging himself (a popular reason given for the origin of the custom), remembered "when skipping was done in nearly all the streets of the town, but when these dangerous motor cars came, they stopped all that; although it is still done in some of the back streets". Sometimes the men turning the ropes expected to be paid a few pence for their efforts. The ropes used at Brighton probably came from the fishing boats, although at other places scaffold ropes, well ropes, clothes lines, and even hop vines were used. Skipping at Brighton came to an end when the forecourt of the open-air fish market was closed with barbed-wire in 1940; it was a minor casualty of the early days of the war.

Other Sussex places where skipping was popular included Hastings, Hove, Southwick, and Lewes. Not far from Brighton, Patcham had a tradition of Good Friday skipping. Here the farm labourers took turns to swing the rope while the rest of the villagers skipped, several at a time, all through the day.

The end of skipping at Brighton seems to have been the reason for the custom surviving into more recent times at Alciston. In the 1940s, a party of skippers, finding their usual skipping ground barred by wartime defences, walked over the hills to Alciston, where they skipped in front of the *Rose Cottage Inn*. In 1954 the *Sussex County Magazine* was able to print two photographs of skipping at Alciston on Good Friday. These showed that, although the long rope and the custom of several people skipping together was still in evidence, most of the participants were children. In a subsequent issue, Stanley Godman of Lewes said that he had witnessed the skipping and was impressed by the spontaneity of the whole affair, in spite of a mass of cars, press photographers, and crowds.

The custom of skipping at Alciston seems to have faded out in the 1960s due to the actions of vandals. Cyril Phillips of Cuckfield told me that he remembered the skipping around midday in the road outside the inn, and that in the afternoon the skippers walked to Berwick Woods to pick primroses and bluebells, before returning home by train to Lewes. One year, some unthinking folk decided instead to help themselves to the narcissi and daffodils belonging to the owner of the inn, and this brought the whole thing to an end.

A conscious effort to revive Good Friday skipping was made at South Heighton in 1954, and again in 1955, when about two hundred people gathered outside the *Hampden Arms* and in addition to skipping and playing marbles, raised nearly £4 (all in pennies) for the children's playing-field fund. An unusual feature of the South Heighton skipping was the Johnny Bell coat, named after the man who revived the custom. The coat was a leather jerkin trimmed with red felt and covered with many bells, which ring as the wearer skips. As one person finishes skipping, the coat is quickly handed over to another, so that the bells are not silent for long.

Good Friday skipping was not confined solely to Sussex, although it seems to have been particularly popular in our county. In addition it has been recorded in Cambridgeshire, Warwickshire, and London. In the neighbouring county of Surrey, it was practised at St Martha's, on the heights overlooking Guildford.

Skipping is a very old pastime, with magical significance, and although Good Friday skipping in Sussex has been linked to the suicide of Judas, the ritual may well extend back to pre-Christian days. You can never be sure that skipping on Good Friday has died out in Sussex. I suspect that it hasn't and that it will pop up somewhere or other at any time. Unlike marbles playing which is by no means extinct, it has not continued or been revived. But there seems no reason why such an excellent and healthy custom should have to die. But remember, to be authentic it must be communal, with at least twenty adult skippers of both sexes joining in when the action really gets under way.

Good Friday skipping at Brighton c.1937-9.

Below: Brighton Fish Market early in this century. The Brighton fishermen used their ropes for skipping here on Good Friday.

Above: Skipping on Brighton Fishermen's beach c.1936-7. Good Friday. *Photo: Mr R. Merrifield*

The Marbles Players

Many people in Sussex will have heard about the marbles games at Battle and Tinsley Green on Good Friday, but a hundred years ago marbles was played all over the county, from Bodiam, Northiam, Saleshurst, and Robertsbridge in the east, through Selmeston, Lewes, Cuckfield, Slaugham, and Horsham, to West Chiltington, Sidlesham, and Rogate in the west.

The Sussex marble season begins on Ash Wednesday and continues until 12 noon on Good Friday, after which no marbles are supposed to be played until the following year – otherwise they can be snatched away with a cry of "smugs!" or some similar magical word.

Horsham's Henry Burstow used to play marbles in West Street with other boys in the 1830s. Although my mother recalled marbles being played by girls at the end of the 19th century it would seem that generally it was played by men and boys, while the girls skipped. Clay marbles were the most common; they cost a penny for anything from forty to a hundred. In some of the Sussex villages, large rings for marble playing were scribed outside one of the main shops.

Sam Spooner, who was born in 1861, was a Sussex marbles champion and one of the first players at Tinsley Green when the games were organized into the championship we know today. According to Sam, marbles was first played at Tinsley Green in the reign of Good Queen Bess, when local lads played for the hand of a rosy-cheeked maid, and it has been played in or around this place ever since. A lovely story, even if it lacks substance.

One of the most successful teams in the early days of the revival was that of the Crawley busmen, who had nicknames like "Killer" Cook, "Brong" Bransden, "Dunnit" Thorp, "Smug" Penfold, "Sparks" Mobsby, and "Brum", the Crawley Terror. As one writer has recorded, they sound more like Chicago gangsters than a marbles team. They were largely responsible for the modern championships.

There were also great postwar teams, such as the Tinsley Green Tigers, the first team to win the championship five times in succession. The captain of the Tigers was George Burberry, who had been playing for a great many years and had the distinction of being the last thatcher to live in Three Bridges.

One of the most accomplished and popular players was George "Pop" Maynard, captain of the Copthorne Spitfires, who was also well known as a great singer of traditional songs. Other members of the Spitfires were Pop's three sons, George Jr., Percy, and Arthur.

As the game is played at Tinsley Green, 49 marbles are placed in a six-foot ring (four marbles for each of the two team's six players, plus one). A line is made in the sand and the two captains then stand over the line and drop their "tolleys" (the shooting marbles) from nose level. The tolley nearest the line wins and goes first. The initial shot is made from the edge of the ring. If a player shoots and stays in the ring without knocking a marble out, his tolley must stay in the ring until the player's next shot. If the tolley is knocked out before his next shot, then he is "killed" and takes no further part in the game. If the player knocks a marble out of the ring and his tolley remains in, he can continue shooting until he misses. The winning team is the one with most marbles, or over half the total number.

Pelham Wait and Frank Anderson, who first played marbles early in this century, revived the

Left: The annual Marbles Championship outside the Greyhound at Tinsley Green in 1946. "Pop" Maynard, 75 years old, is kneeling on the right. *Photo: Mr S. McCarthy*
Far left: Sam Spooner, marble champion of Tinsley Green, passing on some of his skills to a future champion.
Photo: Mr S. McCarthy

Some Sussex Champions

game at Battle in 1948. They played from Mount Street to Abbey Green. The two old players wore Sussex smocks and distributed marbles from a Sussex trug. Frank's smock can be seen in the museum at Battle, together with a collection of marbles.

The Battle game is different to the one played at Tinsley Green. A small circle, one foot in diameter, is chalked on the ground and 15 marbles are spread in it. The five players in each team take it in turn to roll their "bossers" from a line some feet from the ring. If a player knocks a marble from the ring, he carries on shooting until he misses. The first team to knock out eight or more marbles wins the match. A result is obtained from the best of three games. One of the attractions of marbles is that many different games can be played with them, as boys of many generations have discovered.

Not everyone was in favour of marbles on Good Friday. A Sussex vicar, writing in *Notes and Queries* in 1879, observed that his marbles playing parishioners continued their game at the very gate of the church until the last possible moment before the service began, and as soon as it was over they hurried out to resume the game, carrying on for the rest of the day. Even as late as 1948, the vicar at Tinsley Green tried in vain to persuade his parishioners to hold their match on Easter Monday instead of Good Friday. In about 1900 a sensible compromise was found at Streat, where the farm labourers, after performing their essential tasks early in the morning, were given the rest of Good Friday as a holiday on condition that they went to church. They attended the morning service, and then all went out to play marbles, continuing until the evening.

And not only on Good Friday was marbles playing frowned upon. This was a notice exhibited by the Warnham Churchwardens in 1850:

> **Notice:** *Whereas frequent complaints have been made to us of the assemblage of many idle and disorderly persons on Sundays, who molest and otherwise annoy females passing along the Highways of this Parish, and who also play at Marbles and other unlawful games thereon, to the great nuisance of the public. Now we do hereby give notice, that all persons found offending will be punished with the utmost severity of the law.*

Probably this dislike of marbles playing in Sussex was because it was looked upon as a form of gambling. However, marbles in Sussex are still alive and well, and modern-day teams at Tinsley Green rejoice in such names as the Bow Street Fudgers, the Handcross Rebels and the Black Dog Team, from the pub of that name in Crawley.

The Tinsley Green championship is played each Good Friday outside the *Greyhound* pub, in the shadow of Gatwick airport. (Attempts to move the game to the Crawley Sports Centre were unsuccessful.) The greatest compliment that can be paid to a team taking part is that they come for the beer and the fun rather than the silver cup.

Taken in 1949, this photograph shows the annual marble game at Battle, East Sussex. *Photo: Ralph Merrifield*

The Howling Boys

The Howling Boys of Sussex turned out each year to ensure that fruit trees would escape the attention of the evil spirits and provide a satisfactory crop in the coming season. Dressed in an assortment of strange clothes, they would arrive after dark and request permission of the owners of the trees to perform with their cow's horns, drums, and other noise-making implements. Gathering around each tree they would begin with an ancient ditty, something along these lines:

Stand fast root, bear well top,
Pray the Gods send us a good howling crop.
Every twig, apples big,
Every bough, apples enow,
Hats full, caps full, my pockets full too.

A writer in the *Sussex County Magazine* in 1941 recalled that his father, who was born in 1836 at West Chiltington, said that each word was said very deliberately, with the right hand uplifted and circled at the last line. Viscountess Wolseley remembered that sometimes the final line would be changed to "Old parson's breeches full" – a reference to the tithes that the local clergyman once exacted from his parishioners.

The Howling Boys would emphasize the words of the chant with blows on the tree trunk, ending with shouts and hurrahs, and perhaps even firing a gun into the branches of the tree. Sometimes cider would be poured on the roots, although it was more likely to be drunk by the participants at the end of the ceremony.

Writing in 1889, Lady Hurst of Horsham spoke of beating the trees as "a custom nearly or quite obsolete in Sussex". But, of course, like many of these ancient observances it lingered on much longer in some places. We do not know when it originated, although it has been conjectured (with some justification) that it must have pre-Christian roots. In 1669 it was apparently going strong in Horsted Keynes, for the Rev. Giles Moore noted in his diary on 26 December, "I gave the Howling Boys 6d".

Howling Boys usually performed their rites during the twelve days of Christmas, and more especially on Boxing Day. They were always male. They set out in groups rather like carol singers and mummers and expected to be paid for their efforts, in kind if not in cash. A full glass of something all round was the very least a grateful orchard-owner could provide after his trees had been well and truly beaten for another year. Something hot and strong was always appreciated, such as "lamb's wool", made with pulped apples, raw brown sugar, grated nutmeg, a little ginger, and a quantity of strong ale. Obviously, after making a number of calls, each one followed by suitable refreshment, the Howling Boys were in a pretty merry state.

Most of their songs or chants are very similar, but with minor variations from place to place. Arthur Beckett, in his *Adventures of a Quiet Man*, quotes the words of a verse sung by "wastlers" in around 1850:

Good master and good mistress,
a-setting by your fire,
Remember we poor wastlers
have trudged through dirt and mire,
Send out your eldest darter, if you will be so kind,
Send out your eldest darter,
with strong beer and some wine.

The term "Howling Boys", it has been suggested, comes from the Anglo-Saxon word "Yule", although just as good a case can be made that it simply comes from the noise made by the men and lads as they went about their task. Like many old

Left: The Chanctonbury Ring Morris Men wassail the fruit trees at Henfield in January 1980. Photo: Adur Herald

Beating the Trees

ceremonies, it must have started with very serious intent, but it later degenerated into an excuse for a merry evening with perhaps some financial reward thrown in. Many people set great store by the custom, although others probably saw it as an annoyance that had to be endured.

In the 1900s the custom was fast dying out, although at Duncton, near Petworth, it seems to have been carried out with some enthusiasm well into the 1920s. This was probably the last place in Sussex to have seen, and heard, traditional Howlers at work although there have been several revivals in recent years. On Twelfth Night in 1967 the Chanctonbury Ring Morris Men gave the old custom a new lease of life by addressing the apple trees at Tendring in the traditional manner. Since then they have continued with similar ceremonies each year. Their example has been followed by the Broadwood Morris Men, who have visited orchards at Kirdford and, more recently, pubs whose landlords would agree to their apple trees being awakened by chants and dances.

Trees were not the only bearers of a crop to receive the Howling Boys' attention – in some places they also visited the beehives, but detailed knowledge of this activity seems to have passed into oblivion.

The village of Kirdford, where the Morris Men have "Howled" the apple trees on Twelfth Night for many generations.

Stoolball

Often, when I talk about old Sussex pastimes, someone will add the remark that "stoolball is to Sussex as rugby is to Wales". The game is certainly played with great enthusiasm in the county at the present time – there are over two hundred teams playing competitively, many more than in the neighbouring counties of Kent, Surrey, and Hampshire. But as far back as the 15th century the game was being played in many other parts of England. In 1450 parish priests were instructed to prevent the game being played in churchyards (unlike cricket, the game does not require an absolutely level ground). A century later stoolball players in Surrey were in trouble for playing on Sundays. Much of our knowledge of the game in earlier days comes from records of complaints made to magistrates concerning the players' preference for playing stoolball rather than attending church.

The 17th century poet Robert Herrick mentioned stoolball, which has been called the grandmother of cricket as well as the ancestor of rounders and baseball. It has been described by one commentator as "cricket up in the air". The name is said to date from the time when milkmaids stools were used as wickets. Some would even have us believe that a game referred to in the Doomsday Book as "bittle battle" was in fact a version of stoolball. (When, in 1884, a writer advised his readers to go to Telscombe and persuade the rector there to get up a game of stoolball for his especial benefit, he commented that the game itself being old, the older the players are the better.)

The 17th century would seem to have been a very popular time for the game, and Archbishop Laud was worried because "several spend their time in stoolball". By this time the game was as much a woman's pastime as a man's; surprisingly so, as so many other games were purely male preserves. During the 1800s and early in the following century, the game was played very much by women and girls, notably by teams made up of maids from the big estates. The Sussex gentry seem to have encouraged stoolball as a women's game, as did school teachers, and this undoubtedly helped to keep it alive.

Many different spellings of the name have been used over the years, ranging from "stowball" to "stockball". Another name for the game, or at least a version of it, has been used in Sussex. This is "tut" or "tuts". Mrs Langley remembered the former word as the name given to a form of stoolball played between neighbouring villages to the north of Horsham, early in this century.

Stoolball has been played in many different ways at different times. The modern game is played with a board fixed to a post as a wicket; with wooden bats; and balls not quite as hard as cricket balls.

Many older folk remember stoolball being played in Sussex in their youth. Mrs Richter remembers playing it at Plummers Plain when she was in service in 1909. Mrs Chandler, who was in service at Sheffield Park around the same period, had many happy memories of her team, which was made up of servants and others from the big house. They travelled in a horse and cart, wearing their best clothes, for matches against neighbouring villages and, because these were the only times they ever had an opportunity to leave their own village, they looked upon these outings as tremendous treats.

So we have a game, once popular throughout the country, which by the 19th century had fallen out of favour in most places except the southeast

Left: Stoolball. Women playing in Horsham Park 1878. Park House in the background.
Far left: Stoolball at Tarring. Painting by E. Martin.
Photo: Worthing Museum and Art Gallery

"Cricket up in the air."

corner of England and, in particular, Sussex. This must be the reason for the strongly held opinion of so many people that stoolball is purely a Sussex game.

When World War I put a stop to so many things, stoolball might have been one more casualty, never to have reappeared, had it not been for the enthusiasm of one man, Major W.W. Grantham. At that time he was a familiar figure in the county, wearing his Sussex smock and a beaver hat wherever stoolball was played. He researched the game, made a collection of press cuttings on it, and wrote widely about it. His book *Stoolball and how to play it* is, as far as I know, the only book ever written on the sport. The first edition appeared in 1919, and in 1931 he published an enlarged second edition, which includes many references and pictures relating to Sussex.

The title page describes Major Grantham as President of the East Sussex Elementary Schools Stoolball League and Founder of the Stoolball Association of Great Britain. The book contains the rules of the game, hints on playing, notes on bowling, fielding, and batting, and lists of matches and scores. There is even a poem, entitled "The Stoolball Girl", by Dwyer Hand:

Phyllis ever fond of sport, Croquet seldom plays;
Rarely treads the tennis court, yet on summer days
Lissom Phyllis can be seen, freed of hat and frills,
Playing stoolball on the green, near the Sussex hills.

The spark that started Major Grantham on his one-man crusade on behalf of Sussex stoolball came in July 1917, when the war had been raging for three years, and his eldest son returned from France badly wounded. Looking for a sport that wounded men, such as his own son, might be able to play, he hit upon stoolball as the ideal compromise – not as energetic as tennis or cricket, suitable for any age and either sex, and simple to learn and play.

This wartime revival was largely responsible for the popularity of the game today. There is now a national association, based in Sussex. Fierce competition takes place between teams, both women's and mixed, and as far as this corner of England is concerned the game is in a very healthy state. An article in the *Sussex County Magazine* in 1928 pointed out, rightly, that the stoolball revival was one of the few good things to come out of World War I.

We will let Major Grantham provide the last words:

S. *Simple to learn and play.*
T. *The pitch need not be on very short grass.*
O. *One-armed men can become very proficient.*
O. *Old and young can play it.*
L. *Length of each innings can be decided on before beginning.*
B. *Both sexes have proved themselves adept.*
A. *All the year round it can be played.*
L. *Less strenuous.*
L. *s.d. Less expensive.*

A modern match of stoolball. *Photo: Mrs Hobbs*

Wives for Sale

Many weird and wonderful things were sold at fairs and markets in old Sussex, but perhaps the most unusual were married women. For the man – and it was undoubtedly a man's world – this was a not uncommon method of breaking free from a troublesome spouse; and sometimes it may have been welcomed by the woman.

Although not sanctioned by authority, it seems to have been regarded by the working class as a genuine method of quick and easy divorce, and was considered to be legal provided the woman would submit to being led to the market place with a halter round her neck. Readers of Thomas Hardy will be aware that such goings-on happened in places other than Sussex.

It is not clear when the custom began, but as far back as 1790 the *Sussex Weekly Advertiser* printed a full account of a sale at Ninfield, where a man offered his wife in the famous Ninfield stocks. The buyer, who was described as "being in liquor", obtained his bargain for the price of half a pint of gin, but the seller, not wishing to take advantage of his condition, did not attempt to deliver the woman until the following morning. We are told that the buyer was still perfectly happy to receive her, with a halter around her neck, and in the presence of two witnesses. The wife appeared highly delighted over the transaction, and the pair departed "filled with joy". The newspaper commented that it might save a lot of trouble and expense if greater folks used the same method when desiring a divorce. But the catch in the story came a week later, when the paper printed a much shorter note to the effect that the original husband had later repurchased his wife at a higher price. The whole thing has the sound of a bit of drunken tomfoolery.

In the same year a similar thing happened at Lewes, with the original transaction lasting a month, before once again the wife was repurchased for a larger sum. In 1797 a blacksmith from Cliffe disposed of his wife in Lewes market for an undisclosed sum, but in this case there is no record of her being bought back again.

The *Sussex Weekly Advertiser* was again able to report a wife sale in 1799, when in Brighton a man named Staines sold his wife, "by private contract", for five shillings and eight pots of beer, to one James Marten, also of Brighton. Articles of separation and sale were said to have been signed by both parties, and the deed was witnessed by two married couples described as "being under the influence of John Barleycorn".

Some of the best wife-selling accounts are given by Horsham's Henry Burstow in his *Reminiscences*, published in 1911. He tells us that a woman named Smart, the mother of two children, was sold by her husband in about 1820 for three shillings and sixpence. She was bought by a man named Steere from Billingshurst. She had two children by him, but he, like her first husband, found in her characteristics that he could not endure, and sold her again. Her buyer this time was a man named Greenfield, who was apparently made of sterner stuff – he kept to his bargain until the woman's death.

At the Horsham November Fair of 1825, a journeyman blacksmith put his wife up for sale with a halter round her neck. Because she was a good-looking woman she sold for the relatively high sum of two pounds, five shillings; but the purchaser had to agree to take on one of her three children as part of the deal.

Social attitudes were beginning to change by this time, and some of those who witnessed the sale reported it to a magistrate, but the contracting parties disappeared before any action could be taken.

The last case mentioned by Burstow was in 1844, when Ann Holland (known as Pin-Toe Nanny) was led into the market with a halter round her neck, and sold for one pound, ten shillings. To the accompaniment of hisses and boos, she was knocked down to a Mr Johnson of Shipley, who had to sell his watch in order to buy her. She lived with him for a year, during which time she had one child, then ran away, finally marrying a man named Jim Smith, with whom she lived happily for many years.

Although these strange sales normally took place at fairs or markets, the strangely named pub, *The Shoulder of Mutton and Cucumber*, at Yapton was said to be the venue for a sale in 1898, when a local thatcher named Marley obtained seven shillings and sixpence and a quart of beer for his wife. The purchaser was a ratcatcher named White – and there the story ends.

Top right: Lewes Sheep Fair. c.1891. Lewes was one of the places in Sussex where wives were offered for sale by disgruntled husbands. Photo: Sussex Archaeological Society

Right: Wives were sold with halters round their necks at Horsham market. This was when the market had been moved to the Bishopric.

Quoits

Today it is the game of darts that is often associated with public houses; in the 19th and early 20th centuries it was quoits.

The game was played with metal rings, varying in weight, but perhaps of 5, 6, 7, or even 8 pounds each. Quoits may have originated as horseshoes, but in their subsequent form they resembled an inverted saucer, about nine inches in diameter, with a six-inch hole in the centre. Each player had two quoits, which he tossed with a round-arm action, aiming at a "pig" or "peg" in the centre of a clay bed. It was usual to have two beds, not less than four feet square, side by side. Each bed was filled with clay to a depth of about six inches. The iron hub in the centre normally had something white, such as feather, fixed to it as a marker.

The nearest quoit to the centre pig scored, and the winner was the one who reached twenty-one points. It was every player's ambition to land the quoit completely over the pig. This was known as a "ringer" and counted double. The experts could do things like cutting out other quoits near the centre. A "party piece" was to cut a piece of paper held by the centre pig into two halves.

Pub quoits seems to have died out almost completely in Sussex, although two teams play each other on Boxing Day each year at Staplefield.

Collecting memories from the great days of quoits, I found that many of the men recalled their passing with great regret, whereas wives were more than a little relieved when their menfolk stopped spending so much of their time at this, essentially masculine pastime. At Groombridge, Barbara Lee, writing in a little book of memories of village life in the first half of the 20th century, recalled that it was a rough game, often developing into fights between teams taking part. She also commented that it was a skilled game, with the weight of the quoits used varying from player to player according to body weight. The Groombridge Quoits Ground was on the recreation ground, and was a four-foot square made of Blackham clay. Others I spoke to stressed that it was not a game for weaklings or boys. George Attrill of Fittleworth was as renowned for his quoits playing as he was as a cricketer and a drinker.

Not all the quoits rinks were close to pubs, although most of the teams must have had one of the local hostelries as their headquarters. Margaret Chambers, of Seaford, told me that she remembered as a child watching many teams playing on common land between Steyne Road and the sea walls. The pitch had a patch of soft mud at each end, with a seagull's feather stuck in the middle. When each man had thrown, the score was totted up, and the teams changed ends. There were competitions and visiting teams challenged the locals.

I suspect that quite a number of the challenge cups survive. Mrs J.H. Leister, of Lewes, told me that her husband had a cup presented in 1902, with the following inscription on it:

Lewes Quoiting Association Challenge Cup.
Presented by the Mayor of Lewes.
Alderman Major Gates. 1902.

Of course, it was not only cups that were presented as prizes, but also such things as medals, clocks, and salad bowls.

World War I dealt the final blow to the existence of many of the quoits teams, although a few carried on into the 1920s. Mr R.N. Williams was able to give me some memories from his younger days, when he watched games being played at the *Welldiggers Arms*, near Petworth. As he too said, it was not a game for weaklings, each player normally

Quoits from Horsham Museum, giving a very good idea of their shape and feel. They have become pitted and scratched with use.
Photo: Horsham Museum

"Not a game for weaklings"

stripped to the waist and, at a time when men took great pride in their masculinity, this was a great chance to show off to their peers and to their girl friends. Games continued at the *Welldiggers Arms* until the late 1930s, the clay being well looked after and always kept damp so that the quoits would dig in well as they landed.

A team at Rushlake Green was formed, unusually, after World War I. Mr F. Barton, who lived in the village for seventy-odd years, remembers that the teams continued to play until the beginning of World War II. In this area the Quoits League was known as the Hailsham League and matches were played under League rules. But men would play just for fun, or for practice, taking drinks out from the pub while they played.

Quoits Team from the Barley Mow at Selmeston. The photo is undated, but appears to be from late in the last century.
Photo: Mr G. Gutsell

Quoits Team c.1910. Outside Windmill Pub, Portslade.
Photo: B. Banks

Quoits Team outside the Victory Inn, Staplefield in 1913. The game was revived here in modern times, and is played on Boxing Day morning with the same quoits as shown in this photograph.
Photo: Mr R. Ray

Rough Music

Rough music (its more usual Sussex name – others were "skimmington" and "skymington") was once a not uncommon way of expressing disapproval of an offending individual or couple. A crowd would gather, usually after dark, with each person carrying something to make a din – a kettle, saucepan, shovel, or poker, even a footbath full of stones, a bird-scaring rattle, or a set of bells. The "music" was played at the door of the offender's house, which would sometimes mean that the victim as well as the guilty one had to suffer the punishment. We have reports of rough music for the whole of the 19th century from different parts of Sussex – in 1847 at West Hoathly, in 1861 in North Street, Chichester, in 1863 at Arundel.

Sometimes the police would be called to disperse the mob, but often their efforts were in vain. In Chichester in 1864 a great number of men and boys congregated, making a great disturbance with tin cans and kettles, shouting and hooting, and smashing several windows. On the following day the Mayor of Chichester had distributed through the streets a notice pointing out that such disturbances were unlawful and that those taking part in them were liable to punishment. The next evening a further attempt was made to continue the trouble, but the police arrested one of the leaders and succeeded in restoring order.

The most common reason for rough music was a husband beating his wife too severely or a wife beating her husband (as occasionally happened) or having an affair with another man. At Bury a rhyme was sung by the "kangaroo bands";

There is a man lives in this place,
He beat his wife – a sad disgrace,
He beat her black, he beat her blue,
He made her poor bones rattle too.
Now if this man don't mend his manners,
We'll have to send him to the tanners,
And if the tanner don't tan him well,
We'll hang him on a nail in Hell.
And if that nail should chance to crack,
He'll fall upon the Devil's back,
And should the Devil chance to run,
We'll shoot him with his fiery gun. Bang.

The story of the vicar of Amberley and John Pennicott has been told several times. Pennicott was the clarinet player in the Amberley church band and he also led the bands at Henfield and Woodmancote at different times. Although he had lived for 40 years in Amberley village, relations between him and the vicar were not good. Finally, one Sunday, Pennicott and his fellow musicians refused to play for the service, and the vicar shouted from the pulpit, "Are you going to play, or not?" When the answer was an emphatic "No", the vicar replied "Then I am not going to preach". Later, when the service was over, the band came out into the village street and proceeded to the vicarage, where they gave their version of rough music.

At Copthorne, the owner of a cottage was very hard on trespassers and had even peppered one of the villagers with his shotgun. For his pains he was treated to a dose of rough music, with the participants marching up and down in front of his house for some hours.

This seems to be one genuine folk custom that refused to die out completely. Violet Alford, writing in *Folklore* (vol. 70, December 1959), mentions an example at West Hoathly in July 1947, when a well-to-do gentleman had the young men of the village outside his house with rough music for three nights. When the police were called the village lads claimed, "it is our right!"

A modern but timeless view of the old town of Petworth. "Rough Music" was once performed here. *Photo: Gordon Thompson*

The Community's Disapproval

Rough music was not the only way of expressing disapproval or ridicule of members of the community who had misbehaved. Sometimes an effigy of the person would be made and exhibited outside their house, or carried around the streets. These might be accompanied by rough music, or in some cases effigies would be left to convey their own message. Henry Burstow said in his *Reminiscences* that St Crispin's Day (25 October) was the day when anyone who had misbehaved or become in some way notorious during the year was held up to public execration. An effigy of each offender – frequently there would be two together – was hung on the signpost of one or other of the local pubs and left there until 5 November, when they were burnt. One year the effigies were of a man and his wife who had cruelly abused a boy, son of the man and stepson of the woman, by whipping him with stinging nettles. There they hung, each with a bunch of nettles in their hands, until 5 November, when a hostile crowd collected and went to the man's house, assaulted him, and smashed his handcart. For this they were fined £2 each, an amount quickly covered by public subscription.

Mr J. Greenfield, writing about Petworth in days gone by (in *Tales of Old Petworth*, 1976), has several stories about the making of these effigies. He also describes what he calls "a famous skimmington", when one Whit Tuesday, the rough music party dressed at the *Angel*, with one man impersonating the husband, wearing ram's horns on his head, and another man, young, slight and of fair complexion, made up to look like a woman.

The old custom of tarring and feathering some unfortunate who has transgressed the social codes of the community has not completely died out. During my own childhood in the 1930s, I remember one example of summary justice of this kind being carried out upon a young man whose only crime, as far as I could understand, was that he was a trifle effeminate – although I cannot be sure that there was not more to the incident than just that.

A slightly less sinister version of tarring and feathering sometimes accompanies the custom of banging-out, a procedure which is still carried on to the present day. The custom has a very lively existence in the printing trade. At a Haywards Heath firm, four apprentices were banged-out a few years ago, when a disgusting concoction of ink, cat food, and so on was poured over them. In Horsham, not long ago, a printing apprentice who had finished his four-year stint was working away quietly when his colleagues began their version of rough music, building up to a crescendo of sound. This was only a prelude, as they then grabbed the youth, who was placed in a dustbin and held down while a mixture of flour and water, food colouring, wallpaper paste, and various other evil-smelling liquids was poured over him. He was then crowned with a dunce's cap bearing his initials, and pushed around the nearby streets. The custom in the printing trade goes back a very long time, and is said to provide an opportunity to point out to the ex-apprentice the humble part he will still play in the scheme of things, and to instill in him respect for his elders. Apprentice coopers are also likely to be placed in their own barrels, and to suffer the indignity of tarring and feathering. Brides-to-be are also subject to a banging-out ceremony at some workplaces, and although the methods employed are a little less dirty than for the apprentices, the principle is exactly the same.

The Sussex Truffle

Truffles are a type of underground fungi, considered a great delicacy since classical times, and once greatly esteemed in the kitchens and tables of the big houses of Sussex. Although still bought and used on the continent, they appear to have lost favour in this country. In size they measure from one to five inches or, as one man described them, from the size of a small plum to that of a large potato. They have black marbled flesh that looks very like the delicious rum-flavoured confectionery sold under the same name. When in season they have a very strong odour, and possibly because of their elusiveness, have been treated with superstition in the past. It was once believed that they would not continue to grow once someone had looked on them.

Because they are fungi, they have no root or seed, and are difficult to locate, their strong smell being the only clue as to their whereabouts underground. They grow at a depth varying from just below the soil surface to about a foot down, although a few inches down would seem to be the most common. In the 19th century there were men who earned a living as truffle hunters in Sussex, using either dogs or pigs to find the hidden truffles. Dogs were the most popular – pigs, although they sniffed out the truffles well enough, were apt to gobble them up before the hunter could grab the prize (a rope was sometimes tied to one of their back legs, to pull them away from their prize), whereas dogs were content to be rewarded with a piece of truffle-flavour bread.

The most commonly quoted account of Sussex truffle hunting is in Horsfield's monumental *History, Antiquities and Topography of the County of Sussex*. According to Horsfield, the beech woods in the parish of Patching were very productive of the truffle. About forty years earlier, William Leach came from the West Indies, with hogs who were accustomed to hunt for truffles. He spent four years travelling along the coast from Lands End to the mouth of the Thames, searching for the spot where truffles were most abundant. He finally settled on Patching, where he stayed and carried on the business of a truffle hunter until his death. We do not know if he merely dug the truffles or actually cultivated them – propagation is apparently very difficult, and takes several years.

In France and Italy truffles are found in chestnut woods, but in Sussex and other English counties it seems that beech woods have yielded the best crops. Their scent has already been mentioned. Although dogs are normally used to track them down (poodles were popular in France), it has been said that a man lying on the ground can also detect them.

A correspondent in the *Sussex County Magazine* in 1931 recalled an old Irishwoman named Mary Hack who sold truffles she found under the beech trees in Patching. She would tell no one where the truffles were and apparently her secret died with her.

Patching was by no means the only place in Sussex where truffles were found. In the 1930s an old man named Oliver hunted truffles, with the help of several dogs, on the Goodwood Estate. He seems to have been one of several truffle hunters who worked in this area at different times.

Gilbert White, in his *Natural History of Selborne*, refers to a truffle hunter who called on him with several large truffles in his pockets. He said that these had been found in narrow hedgerows and the skirts of coppices. Half-a-crown a pound was the price he asked.

There were many ways in which the humble

truffle could be cooked, and old recipe books feature several recipes that include them. Once known as the Diamonds of the Kitchen they would now be difficult to buy, except perhaps in tins emanating from across the Channel.

Perhaps because of the use of pigs in searching for them, truffles have sometimes been called pig-nuts, but the true pig-nuts are the tubers at the base of the root of an umbelliferous white flower, *Conopodium majux*. Also called earth nuts or peg-nuts, these were a rather humble delicacy, loved by small boys in the early years of this century, when anything edible and free was highly prized. Mr S. Neve of Hassocks recalled that when he was a boy in Ninfield he and his friends could find the plants without difficulty and would then dig out the roots with a penknife. The nuts were found some four to six inches down, at the base of the roots. Only two or three might be discovered in one session, and great care was needed to avoid breaking the root. He commented that parents were not keen on this method of supplementing the diet, as they believed that it might give the boys worms. Mrs M. Bryant of Shipley also remembered them, although she called them groundnuts. With her cousins she found them in the churchyard woods. They were very sweet to eat, but only edible in the spring. Mr C. Potter of Horsham remembered them as peg-nuts and recalled pulling them out of the ground in the Jews Meadows – the fields where the fairs and circuses were set up at different times of the year. The tops resembled carrots, and he described the taste of the nuts as "lovely".

Below: The Goodwood Estate. In the early part of this century there were several areas on the estate where truffles might be found.

Virgins' Wreaths

The American writer Washington Irving described, early in the 19th century, an ancient English custom that was still in being in country areas. This is what he wrote:

There is a most delicate and beautiful rite observed in some of the remote villages of the south, at the funeral of a female who has died young and unmarried. A chaplet of white flowers is borne before the corpse, by a young girl nearest in age, size and resemblance, and is afterwards hung up in the church over the accustomed seat of the deceased. These chaplets are sometimes made of white paper, in imitation of flowers, and inside of them is generally a pair of white gloves. They are intended as emblems of the purity of the deceased, and the crown of glory which she has received in heaven.

Washington Irving refers to "the south" although most evidence seems to suggest that the charming custom of virgins' garlands was mostly found in the north of England. William Howitt, writing in *The Rural Life of England* (1862), records that these garlands were used in his own native village in Derbyshire and also at Witton-Gilbert, near Durham. He also says that the emblems were originally real flowers (lilies and roses) and that the gloves were of white kid. The garlands were placed on the coffin during the funeral procession and were then hung in the church.

The Lindfield local historian Helena Hall wrote in the *Sussex County Magazine* in 1939 that she had seen some fine virgins' garlands in St. Mary's Church, Abbotts Ann, near Andover in Hampshire. Here the garlands were made from white paper and were in the form of a crown with two arches above a circle, from which four or five white paper gloves were suspended. She thought that the gloves were gauntlets representing a challenge to anyone questioning the good character of the deceased. The garland was hung from a small wand, and borne by two maidens dressed in white, at the head of the funeral procession. At the grave it was placed on the coffin, and afterwards carried to the church and hung so that all would pass under it. She saw about forty garlands hung along both sides of the nave, the earliest date being 1740 and the latest 1919.

Gilbert White mentions virgins' garlands as being hung in churches in his time (1720-1793). He recalled having seen the parish clerk's wife cutting, in white paper, the resemblance of gloves and ribbons to be twisted in knots and roses, to signify chastity. He also mentioned that many garlands remained in the church at Faringdon.

Although the custom was possibly observed in many Sussex churches in the past, the only one of which we seem to have actual evidence is Alfriston. Here, at the end of the 18th century, Garlands were hung in the church after being borne on the coffin of a young woman. They remained in the church until they withered, as emblems of mortality.

Florence Pagden in her *History of Alfriston*, first published in 1899, wrote that the custom was observed in that village a hundred years earlier. She also quotes the *Antiquarian Repertory*, in which the wreaths were described in some detail:

The lower rim was made of a broad circlet of wood, wherunto was fixed at the sides two other hoops, crossing each other at the top at right angles; they were covered with artificial flowers, dyed horn and silk. Between the hoops hung white paper cut in the form of gloves, with age, name, etc of the deceased inscribed thereon, together with strips of various coloured paper or ribbon, intermixed with gilded or painted empty shells of blown eggs, or other ornament, suggestive of the bubbles and bitterness of life; some had a solitary hour glass as an emblem of mortality.

The same writer also says that the garlands were used at the funerals not only of young girls but also of widows who had had only one husband.

In Augustus Hare's book, *Sussex*, published in 1894, he gives the information about the garlands in Alfriston Church, and adds that a few years before there were as many as seventy hanging there at the same time. Most authorities suggest that the garlands remained in the church for a year, although this last reference would suggest that they remained at Alfriston for a much longer time.

Although the wreaths are usually referred to as virgins' or maids' garlands, they were sometimes used at the funerals of young unmarried men, when the circumstances appeared to merit it.

Alfriston Church, where the custom of Virgins' Wreaths was carried on in past centuries.

Here be Dragons

Folklore provides us with many dragon legends, and Sussex has its fair share. As well as the most famous, that of St Leonard's Forest, there is the dragon that once dwelt in the depths of the Knucker Hole at Lyminster, near Arundel. The hole is actually a small, deep pool of clear water, fed by a spring, which, according to local belief, has never been known to run dry. The pool was once reputed to be bottomless, and even when the locals took the ropes from the six bells of Lyminster church, and tied them together, they failed to touch the bottom. However, modern soundings have spoilt this part of the story by proving that it is quite possible to make contact with the bottom.

The basic legend is of a very fierce monster of tremendous size, partly like a serpent, and partly in the shape of a woman. Like all genuine dragons it had wings, and was in the habit of swooping down on the farmers' beasts and carrying them back to its lair. Around the pool there was an accumulation of bones, covering the banks. After suffering the attentions of this dreadful animal for many years, the people who lived in the area sent a deputation to the King, begging him to take some action to rid them of the evil. After much thought, the King decided that because the dragon was so greatly feared, he would have to offer a really exceptional reward to anyone brave enough to stand against it. He therefore offered the hand of his only daughter to the man who would slay the dragon, and because she was very beautiful there was no shortage of young men willing to try their luck. The first was a brave knight, who donned his armour and sought the monster in its den. But no sooner had he arrived at the pool, than the dragon seized him in its coils and crushed him to death.

The next was a miller, who decided to try a plan which owed more to cunning than bravery. He took with him a bag of flour, determined to throw it into the dragon's eyes, so blinding it and rendering it open to attack. Somehow the plan misfired, and the miller was not seen again.

At some point in the story the people of Lyminster decided to try their own solution. They made a very large and heavy plum pudding, skewered it on a long pole, and offered it to the dragon. The greedy beast gulped it down and choked to death on it and the villagers then chopped their tormentor into little pieces – or that is one ending to the story.

The more common tale concerns a local lad by the name of Jim Pulk or Jim Puttock. The stories that mention Jim are all agreed on one point – that he dispatched the dragon without too much difficulty, although there are variations in the way in which this was done. Sometimes we are told that he fought the beast with a sword and killed it in the conventional manner. Alternatively, the pudding is linked with the brave Jim, who is supposed to have obtained a huge pot from the blacksmith, flour from the miller, and the wood for a huge fire from the woodmen. Making the biggest pudding that was ever seen, he had it carried to the dragon on a timber tug, and the hungry monster swallowed it up – horses, tug, and all. Of course it gave it tremendous indigestion, and while it was rolling about in agony, Jim was able to cut off its head with an axe.

As in all good stories, Jim married the King's daughter, and they lived happily ever after. And their descendants may still be found living in this part of Sussex.

As proof that Jim did really exist, his grave, covered with a slab of Horsham stone, used to be in the graveyard of Lyminster church. The slab was

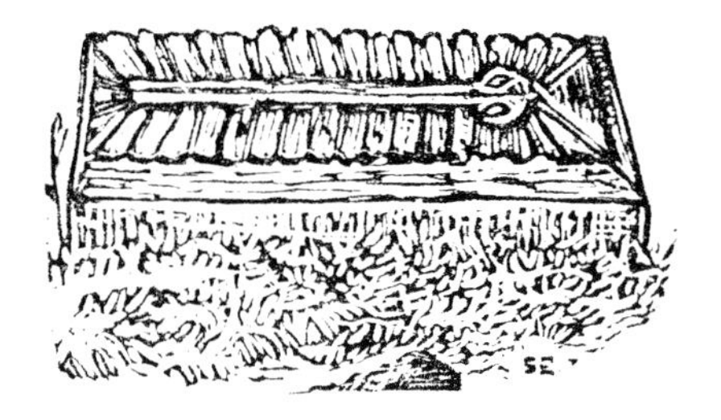

The gravestone of the local boy who killed the Knucker.

later moved from the churchyard into the church itself, and there it may be seen today, next to the font. The decoration on the stone may be interpreted as a full-length cross superimposed on a background of oblique ribbing. This has been likened to a sword laid across the ribs of a dead dragon, although if this is so, then it fits more neatly with the knightly dragon-slayer, rather than our local lad, who used an axe.

There is an interesting sidelight to the version of the tale that has the townsfolk skewering the pudding on to a long pole; in East Africa they once killed crocodiles by thrusting large lumps of meat down their throats in the same way. It has been suggested that this points to the Knucker monster being a crocodile-like prehistoric creature.

There are many explanations offered for the origin of the name of the monster. One of the most logical is that originally the name was spelt "Nucker" and that it comes from Nicor (pronounced "nickor"), the old English name for a water monster.

Another interesting theory concerning this strange beast is that it may have been a great sea eagle. These birds weigh anything up to 14lb and have a wing-span of up to 10ft. They are credited with being able to carry off small animals and even babies. The water monster of the Knucker Hole is supposed to have possessed wings, so the eagle theory may not be too far-fetched.

In the 1980s concern was expressed by local parish councillors over the condition of the ancient Knucker Hole, and it was agreed that it should be cleaned up and made more attractive. Once again the stories of the Knucker and how it was slain were re-told, showing that a good legend never disappears whilst there are local folk to remember it.

Lyminster Parish Church early in this century. The local farmer's boy who is credited with having killed the Knucker, is said to be buried near to the church door.

Photo: Miss D. Hall

The Black Princess

St Leonard's Forest, close to Horsham, has associated with it many legends and items of curious lore. Elsewhere in this book I have mentioned the Devil and the Forest, but these references by no means exhaust the supply of fascinating stories that exist concerning this relatively small piece of wooded land, which was once part of the vast ancient forest of Anderida, described by the Venerable Bede in 731 as "thick and inaccessible".

The best known of all the Forest legends are those telling of the dragon that once dwelt there. Or perhaps there were really several dragons, as some of the stories must have originated in very early times when many strange beasts lived in this inaccessible area. The dragon legends were given a new lease of life in 1614, when a pamphlet was published telling of a "strange serpent or dragon" said to be living at that time within the Forest to the great annoyance of the local residents.

Coming up to slightly more modern times, there are the stories of the Black Princess, who lived on the edge of the Forest from 1805, dying at the age of 81 in Horsham. She was not really a princess, and certainly not black, but she was a Persian aristocrat, known locally as Mrs Helena Bennett – an anglicized form of her husband's name, which was de Boigne. He was a French general who soon after his arrival in England left his wife in a house near Colgate and married the daughter of the French ambassador in London.

Helena, left to her own devices, appears to have become something of a recluse, and little about her has appeared in local histories. Most of our knowledge of her seems to have come from shadowy tales told by the ordinary folk who lived nearby. They were well aware of her generosity to those in need, and perhaps were also just a little bit in awe of her.

In spite of her original background, she was a Roman Catholic, and is said to have attended mass in Horsham each Sunday, which at that time was celebrated in a cottage that stood between West Street and Springfield Road. Strangely enough, though she was buried in a grave, which is still visible, on the right-hand side of the path leading to the main door of the parish church of St Mary the Virgin, in the Causeway, Horsham. The grave is sited north-south, according to Moslem custom. As Miss Audrey Robinson says in her book on Shelley and his links with Horsham, "a truly ecumenical burial".

Many other tales of the Forest are connected with smugglers, who, during the heyday of this activity, utilized the cover provided by the forest trees to hide their illegal merchandise. Mr Aldridge of New Lodge remembered that when he was a boy it was no uncommon thing for thirty or forty fully armed men to ride up the avenue to the house, to be given supper in the servant's hall – an example of the sort of blackmail that inhabitants of lonely unprotected houses were obliged to pay. Lady Hurst, who quotes Mr Aldridge in her *History and Antiquities of Horsham*, also tells us that the smugglers would borrow horses from the stables, use them, groom them, and put them back. We can thus see that it was very much to the advantage of these gentlemen to keep ordinary folk away from their night-time activities, by spreading as many horrific tales about the area as they possibly could. Such was the story of the headless horseman, who was said to pounce on the horse of any unaccompanied rider who was unwise enough to venture into the depth of the Forest after nightfall. Chapter and verse were given to this story by the addition of the detail that the phantom rider was Squire Paulet (or Powlett), whose grave is at West Grinstead, although no reason is ever given as to why this gentleman should act in such an unsocial fashion. Just to bring this story up to date, I was told by a lady at one of my talks that her husband had seen a headless figure standing beside one of the Forest ponds, when according to her account he knew nothing of the headless-horseman stories.

A much earlier item of Forest lore comes from Andrew Borde's *Boke of Knowledge*, where he wrote: "In the Forest of St Leonard in Southsex, there doth never singe nightingale, although the foreste rounde about in tyme of the years is replenished with nightingales". No less a person that St Leonard himself is supposed to have decreed that in the Forest "Ye Adders ne'er sting, nor ye Nightingales sing". A more down-to-earth theory for the apparent scarcity of nightingales within the Forest is that when the Wealden iron industry flourished, so many trees were felled to feed the furnaces that the birds forsook this part of the county. Certainly the iron masters were once very busy within the area of the Forest, as is evidenced by the several hammer ponds which now add to the attractiveness of this part of Sussex. One of these ponds is known locally as Hawkins' Pond, which was said to be the name of a leader of a gang of smugglers.

Now the remains of the once-proud Forest are a delight to walkers and nature lovers. The latter can enjoy the many plants and other forms of natural life which abound, including the beds of lily of the valley, which a pleasing tradition tells us mark the spots where the saint spilt his blood fighting the dragon.

One of the roads leading into St. Leonard's Forest, near Horsham.

The stone marking the grave of "The Black Princess" close to the entrance to Horsham Parish Churchyard. The inscription has been almost rubbed away.

"Old Scratch"

Sussex folk refuse to take the Devil seriously. Almost all the stories about him (and there are many) show him in an inferior, or even ridiculous, light. Our names for him are either rather condescending (Old Man and Poor Man) or just plain silly (Old Harry, Old Scratch, or Mr Grimm). Sussex folklore abounds in stories showing how much more clever and resourceful the Wealden folk are than their devilish adversary. This is shown completely in our two best-known stories featuring the Prince of Darkness. The first concerns Satan's attempt to drown the little churches of the South Downs in one single night, by digging a huge trench to allow the sea to engulf them. He started at Poynings, but disturbed an old woman, who set a candle behind a round sieve in her window, so that the Devil would mistake it for the rising sun. Unable to work after sunrise, he had to give up with his self-appointed task uncompleted. The earth that he had removed provided the mounds that we now know as Chanctonbury, Cissbury, and Mount Caburn. A larger lump became the Isle of Wight.

The second story is about a mile-long avenue of trees in St Leonard's Forest, which is said to be the site of a memorable race between a Sussex smuggler, Mike Mills (or Mick Miles), and the Devil. Of course the Devil was the loser, although some say that the smuggler collapsed and died shortly afterwards. The race track has refused to grow anything except weeds since that day.

There are several stories about St Dunstan and the Devil. An old rhyme has us believe that:

Saint Dunstan, so the story goes,
Caught old Satan by the nose,
He tugged so hard and made him roar,
That he was heard three miles and more.

St Dunstan liked to practise the craft of blacksmithing, and one day when so engaged he was visited by Satan disguised as a beautiful woman. The saint spotting a cloven hoof beneath the silken gown, grabbed his visitor by the nose, utilizing his red-hot pincers. The Devil in anguish flew to Tunbridge Wells, plunging his burning nose into the waters there, thus providing the town with its famed chalybeate springs.

Another story concerning St Dunstan tells of how the Devil continually moved Mayfield church, so that the saint who lived nearby had to push it back into position with his shoulders. Even when the original wooden building was replaced with a stone one, the Devil would move the stones each night during the building process.

There are many stories about churches in Sussex being interfered with by the Devil during their construction. One of the best known is about the Church in the wood at Hollington, near Hastings, which was originally to be built in a more accessible place, but because the builders found their work disturbed and the building materials moved each night, they had to give in and build in the middle of a wood – one example of the Devil having his way.

One of our greatest Sussex eccentrics, Jack Fuller of Brightling, was said to have been buried in a triangular tomb, wrapped in an iron chain, and with broken glass strewn around, so that "When the Devil comes to claim his own, he will end up by cutting his feet".

Several Sussex beliefs promise that Old Scratch can be made to appear, and in some cases provide a basin of soup, if you run around a certain object, usually seven times. Sometimes the task is made more difficult, by the specification that this must be done backwards. This belief is associated with

Mayfield village early in this century. Mayfield attracted several stories concerning the Devil.

Chanctonbury Ring, when the run must be carried out on Midsummer's Eve. Sometimes the promise is attached to a certain tomb or grave or even a tree, as at Kingston Buci.

Sometimes it seems difficult to get away from the Devil in Sussex, as there are so many geographical landmarks with his name attached. Thus we have Footprints, Jumps, Books, Grave, Lanes, Holes, Bog and Frying Pan, to name just a few. Natural history also provides several devilish allusions. Convolvulus is called Devil's Weed, Satan's Snuff Boxes are a certain type of toadstool on the South Downs, and stinging nettles are known as Naughty Man's Playthings – the Naughty Man being one more name for the Devil.

We have by no means exhausted the possibilities of becoming implicated with the Devil as far as Sussex traditional lore is concerned. If you cut your nails on Sundays, then he will chase you all the rest of the week. Keeping horse brasses in the house will attract the Evil One, but at least keep him from other mischief. When the son becomes stronger than the father, then he should give up work, or the Devil will be tempted to claim him. And, of course, most Sussex children know that they should break the bottoms of boiled eggs after eating them, otherwise the Devil will use them as boats.

Another minus for Mr Grimm was his attempt to destroy the Blue Scabious on the Downs, on account of their healing properties. Naturally he failed.

And lastly we must not forget the famous Sussex Whistling Song, which tells the story of an old farmer who was cursed with a shrewish wife. One day the Devil came to the man when he was ploughing and offered to take his wife back to Hell with him. The farmer accepted with gratitude, and away they went – Satan carrying the woman on his back. But the Devil found her more than a match for him and after a short while he returned her to her husband with the remark "I have been a tormentor the whole of my life, but I never was tormented till I met your wife". The title of the song refers to a jaunty whistling tune that provides a chorus to the verse lines.

Hollington Church in the Wood, near Hastings. One of the Sussex churches which suffered from the unwelcome attentions of Old Scratch during construction.

Wise Women and Witches

Sussex witches can be divided into two sorts – wise women, who were the white (or good) kind, and the others who may be termed black, although I doubt if the term was ever actually used by the folk around them. Of course there was no hard and fast distinction, and in some cases it must have been a little difficult to tell one from the other.

My grandmother on my mother's side was very much a wise woman, with cures for warts and other ailments available to all and sundry, and the ability to tell fortunes by the tea leaves, or character by handwriting. People like her must have been very popular, and very useful, when a visit to the doctor was a very expensive business not to be undertaken except in extreme cases. Many people will have their own memories of such white witches either in the family, or living nearby. In 1981, *Sussex History* included a reference to the wise woman of West Chiltington, Elizabeth Spooner. She was born in 1804 and became known as the local wise woman on account of the herbal remedies with which she treated the sick and her skill in dyeing fabrics with her own process using herbs. At the same time she was a very religious woman, so was by no means to be considered a witch in the popular sense. A little different was widow Blackman, remembered by John Hailsham in his book on life in Lindfield (*Idlehurst* 1898). The widow was described as mean and crafty, and in her later years merely a ghost of a witch, with only the power to wish away warts.

Rather more sinister are the stories of what were seen as genuine witches, with supernatural powers, such as the ability to change into hares. Sussex witch-lore is full of stories of female witches who having become hares in order to carry out their evil deeds were then seized by a hound at the moment of escape. Later the witch was observed limping, or rubbing the part of her body corresponding to that which had been nipped by the dog. Mother Digby of Harting was one witch who was chased by the squire's hounds while she was a hare, one of them almost holding her by the hind quarters as she reached her front door.

Horses seemed to have a fascination for witches, many of whom were credited with some very strange powers over cart-horses, causing them to stop at certain places whatever steps the carters took to avert these evil powers. A witch from Wisborough Green was blamed when the horses in a particular stable were found in the morning with their manes tangled. In cases such as this further trouble could be prevented by fastening a fag-hook with a sharp edge overhead. Cold steel was supposed to be the one thing feared by a witch, and most recipes for averting the attention of witches mention the use of steel or iron in some way. A carter who claimed to know all about witches and their spells used his knife to cut notches in the spokes of his wagon wheels when the horses refused to move outside the cottage of a known witch. This was followed by a scream, as the woman rushed out of her front door with blood streaming from gashes in her hands, one for each of the notches on the wheels.

Belief in witches and their powers lingered on, long after legal recognition of them had ceased. George Attrill of Fittleworth told me of a witch in his village who was shunned by most of the other village women – but not by his mother who was evidently a little more courageous, or perhaps more enlightened, than the others. This must have been around the turn of the century, but such beliefs were still fairly common at that time. The *Sussex*

Some "White Witches" were also skilled in other "alternative" occupations, such as herb-doctoring and dowsing. Here is what could almost be described as an advertisement for George Roberts, water diviner, of Henfield.

White and Black Magic

Archaeological Collections for 1919 mention a woman of 73 living in East Sussex who had a profound belief in witchcraft. She was in the habit of boiling pins in urine and she stopped up all the cracks in her cottage – all to avoid the attentions of the local witch, who in this case was a man. The quarterly *Notes and Queries* of the Sussex Archaeological Society carried in May 1933 a report of a man of over 80 in West Sussex who got very excited if anyone derided witchcraft as "rubbish". He told of the bewitching of animals, particularly a farmer's horse which was "overlooked" by a witch so that it became helpless. "Why, it couldn't even die. They got a gun and shot it through the head, but even then it couldn't die. It did not die till they got her to let it die". He went on to tell how he himself had seen an old woman who was reputed to be a witch vanish, to be replaced by a hare that ran through a hole in the hedge. All this from an old man who had no book learning and knew nothing of the belief prevalent all over Europe that a witch when trying to escape can turn into a hare.

In January 1935 there was sold at Stevens' Auction Rooms, King Street, Covent Garden, what was stated to be the skeletal hand of Mary Holt, who was hanged at Pulborough in Sussex, nearly 200 years before. It was said that the hand had been used to cure all diseases. It was once believed that a murderer's hand could be used to cure certain diseases, but in this case it was said that Mary Holt had been a witch, and was hanged for this crime. The Horsham historian, William Albery, felt that this could not have been true, as the last witch executed by hanging in Sussex was in 1575, when Margaret Cooper of Kirdford suffered this penalty for bewitching Henry Stoner.

The last recorded indictment for witchcraft in Sussex was in 1680, when Alice Nash was accused of bewitching Elizabeth Slater, aged 2½ years, and Anne Slater, aged 5½ years, both of whom died. She was acquitted and discharged. Sussex was in fact far less severe on its witches than many other counties, with only 33 indictments, and one execution.

Many different cures and charms against witchcraft were in use. Apart from the boiling of pins mentioned previously, animals "hearts" pierced with pins were also used, and household utensils were marked with "Witche's charms" to deter unwelcome use.

A lifetime of collecting old Sussex photos has failed to produce a real witch – but here is the next best thing, c.1909, from Brighton.

The Cokelers

In 1981 I was privileged to visit two charming ladies in Warnham, who told me that they were part of a tiny group of people who once numbered around 2,000. They are commonly called Cokelers, although they dislike this nickname, and prefer to be known as Christian Dependants, signifying that they depended upon Christ for everything in life.

This unusual sect was founded in Sussex over a century ago by John Sirgood, a shoemaker and self-taught preacher, who was born in Avening, Gloucestershire, in 1821. During the 1840s he moved to London and in 1850, feeling a call to go and preach in the countryside, he set out with his wife, and all their belongings in a wheelbarrow. Sometimes when she was weary, his wife rode in the barrow, and John pushed her as well as all their worldly goods. When they reached Loxwood on the edge of West Sussex, he decided that this was the place to stop, and he and his wife found lodging in the village. One is reminded a little of the legend of St Cuthman of Sussex, and how he wheeled his mother in a barrow, until the accident of a broken wheel caused him to end his journey at Steyning.

Unlike the saint, John Sirgood did not build a church, but held prayer meetings in farm labourers' cottages, soon attracting half of the local working population to his assemblies. Previously he had been a member of a sect called the Peculiar People, and as they believed in faith healing, it was not long before he gained a reputation as a healer. He was even credited with having raised someone from the dead, although there is no evidence that he ever claimed miraculous powers of this sort.

Soon his followers formed themselves into a group, to which the name Cokelers was applied by most outsiders. The reason for the name has never been determined, although the most popular theory is that it was because they drank cocoa rather than beer or spirits at their meetings. Certainly many adherents travelled long distances to attend the prayer meetings on Sundays, and so stayed the whole day, bringing with them their mid-day meal, and partaking of a hot drink, which may well have been cocoa. Other theories are that their first meetings were held in a place called Cokeler's Field or in a part of Loxwood known as Cokkeg.

They were closely allied to Quakers in their outlook on life. Their meetings had no set form, and consisted of Bible readings, unaccompanied hymn singing, and personal testimony. In their daily lives they believed in moderation, with little care for worldly goods or entertainment. Their houses were not ornamented with pictures or nick-nacks, and even flowers were not popular, except in the fields and gardens. Marriage, while not forbidden was not encouraged, and they had no marriage service of their own. Any member of the sect who wished to marry did so in the local parish church, where in many cases they were made welcome by the vicar, who realized that although they were not regular churchgoers they were good Christians.

Their attitude towards one another was of kindness and generosity at all times, and much of this gentleness spilled over into their dealings with those who did not share their religious views. In fact most of their neighbours held the Cokelers in considerable esteem. Not so the local landowners and farmers, who in many cases disliked anything that smacked of unorthodoxy. By 1861 so many of the locals had joined the sect that the following letter was sent to John Sirgood:

> *Mr. Sirgood – Sir, I went to your house on Thursday evening for the purpose of giving you the enclosed notice, but found you holding one of your unlawful*

The Christian Dependants' chapel in Loxwood. Note the absence of an altar, crucifix or any kind of ornamentation.

A Gentle Sect

meetings. I am glad I did this because I have now myself witnessed two of these unlawful assemblies there, and could without difficulty procure your conviction in two penalties and these two could probably be easily multiplied. It is a very general opinion that your illegal proceedings have been allowed to go far enough, and that it is quite time they should be controlled.

However, most of this seems to have been hot air, and no action to stop John Sirgood's meetings was actually taken. The local employers of labour could however sack their workers when they wished, and in some cases this was done, even when a tied cottage went with the employment. At the same time the young girls who were in service found themselves forbidden to leave their places of employment to attend the meetings. To obviate all these difficulties, it was decided to set up a shop and mill where members of the community could live and work unhindered by outside influences. Because the Cokelers were honest and very hardworking the commercial enterprise increased and flourished and became a focal point for the movement.

By the time John Sirgood died in 1885, it was estimated that there were at least 2,000 Christian Dependants in Sussex, and beyond. By this time there were flourishing communities at Northchapel, Warnham, Lords Hill, Kirdford, and even Chichester and Hove. But without the impetus of the founder the sect began to dwindle, and by 1900 only around 900 remained. Very few new adherents joined, as there was no attempt to persuade others to become followers. With few marriages, naturally there were few young families. But a hard core of the brethren continued, and during the 1920s and 1930s the chapels on Sundays and the shops on weekdays continued to function very efficiently.

By 1981, the two Warnham ladies told me, there were only four Christian Dependants left in Warnham. Once there had been a chapel and a large shop that traded as Lindfield Luff, selling almost anything that one could think of, including its own brand of crockery – examples of which may still be found in local homes. At Loxwood, where the sect was founded, the chapel, shop, and all the other commercial enterprises had passed into other hands, and but a small group of the community remained.

On a visit to Canada I met some of the Menonite people, and because of their appearance and outlook on life, I was struck by the feeling that these could be very much as our own Sussex Cokelers might be today, if they had continued to flourish and to multiply, instead of fading away as they have done. Sussex is that much poorer without these gentle people.

Loxwood, the village which saw the start of the religious sect known as the Cokelers.

Taxidermist's Tableaux

Few people would disagree that the strangest museum in the county was that started by Walter Potter in 1861 when he was 26 years old. His sister had a picture book telling the story of "The Death and Burial of Cock Robin". This gave Walter the inspiration to produce a portrayal of the story within a glass case, utilizing no less than ninety-eight specimens of stuffed birds. The case was exhibited in a summer house behind his father's inn, and many people came to admire the unusual display. Of course this was the time when taxidermy was a much admired skill, and stuffed birds and animals graced many drawing rooms and bar parlours. Walter Potter obviously had a talent in this direction, and his original effort brought forth many orders for stuffed creatures from neighbours and friends.

His business, for such it had become, was moved into a specially erected building in Bramber's main street; by 1880 it had blossomed into a full-scale museum and the exhibits were moved into an even larger building nearby.

His next tableau after "Cock Robin", again inspired by a book of nursery rhymes, was "The Babes in the Wood". The church and castle in the background added local interest to the scene, although Norfolk is usually the county associated with this story. Other similar tableaux followed – "The Kittens' Tea and Croquet Party", "The Lower Five or Rats' Den", "The Rabbits' Village School" and several others. They all included young animals expertly stuffed and placed in human-like poses. As well as the tableaux, a vast amount of other strange material was added to the museum – old musical instruments, ox goads, engravings by Gustave Doré, a model of the entrance to Brighton station, cannon balls from Bramber Castle, and much more besides. All this in addition to a great many single stuffed animals, including some freaks, such as a lamb with two heads and a hen with four legs. Many of the animals came from the countryside close by, or from local farms. There was however not a single black cat in the museum, because these were thought to be associated with witches.

The collection was certainly strange, and fascinating in a slightly repellent way – at least to my eyes when I viewed it in later years. There was also a strange aroma associated with the museum, although none of these points appear to have worried the many people who visited the collection in its earlier days.

A guidebook from the early part of this century described it as "a kind of bird and animal Madame Tussaud's". Admission was stated to be "two pence; children one penny. Ladies and Gentlemen their own generosity". E.V. Lucas commented in 1904, "Bramber possesses a humorist in taxidermy, whose efforts win more attention than the castle".

In the museum one could purchase a sixpenny guide, which gave a brief history of the collection, and a detailed list of all the exhibits. In it there is a picture of the originator, Walter Potter, showing a sombre, bearded man in dark clothes, looking rather like the archetypal Victorian clergyman. There is also an interesting sketch of the interior of the museum by Walter Goetz, in which the exhibits cover the floor, walls, ceiling and beams, giving a very claustrophobic effect.

In addition to the little guidebook, picture postcards showing the tableaux were sold, as well as some reproductions of rather odd letters. These cost a penny. "A Singular Love Letter", was supposedly written on 9 May 1864 by a lad named

Charles, of Bishop's Waltham, to a young woman living in London. Her name was Emma, although he spelt it "Hammer". In it he asks her to marry him, and promises he will always "lick" her as long as he lives. He also promises her a Valentine, which he expresses as "waltime". Another penny letter was also a romantic epistle, but only if you read alternate lines. If the letter was read through in a normal way, the sentiments were all of dislike, and even hatred.

This fascinating period piece continued to attract visitors until as recently as 1970, when the widow of the owner, Mr Eddie Collins (the grandson of the founder) decided to put the property up for sale. The premises then became a museum of Smokiana, everything connected with tobacco and smoking. For a time Walter Potter's collection was housed in an even smaller museum in Arundel High Street, having been purchased by Mr James Cartland, the Arundel local historian.

Perhaps it is easy to look a trifle condescendingly at the folk who flocked to view Mr Potter's strange collection in its heyday. But the nature films and splendid photography that we take for granted today were not available to our Victorian forebears. Walter Potter described himself as a naturalist as well as a taxidermist, and obviously he saw nothing wrong in using his skill in the latter craft to bring nature into the lives of the many who visited his museum, however odd his methods may seem today.

Above: Potters Museum at Bramber in its heyday.
Photo: Mr C.W. Cramp

Right: One of the many strange exhibits at Potters Bramber Museum. "The Rats' Party" included a number of genuine stuffed rats in human poses.

Tunnels and Secret Passages

Most people are fascinated by secret passages and tunnels, and stories concerning them can be found in every corner of the county. It is never difficult to find someone to tell a good tale about a local tunnel, but always much more difficult to locate anyone who has actually been in one – it is always very much the "My sister's father-in-law knew a man who could have told you a thing or two...".

The beautiful old town of Arundel possibly has more tunnel stories that most other Sussex towns, perhaps because the ground is mainly chalk, so it would not be too difficult to excavate. One story tells of a secret room, with an entrance covered by carpet, in the drawing room of the castle. From a false wall in this chamber there is supposed to be a tunnel that runs for an unknown distance. A man and a dog once set out to discover the end of the tunnel, but were never seen again – or so the story goes. Or you may prefer another version of the tale, which says that the dog emerged alone about five miles away two weeks later.

There is also said to be a tunnel from Maltravers Street to Tarrant Street, and another under the *Eagle*, big enough to take a dray. More certain is a tunnel from the Castle Gardens to Anne Howard Gardens. This was said to be a disused apple store – a typically mundane explanation for an underground chamber. Smugglers enter into many of these Arundel stories, as indeed they do in tunnel tales from other places.

The most written-up Arundel tunnel is one that was said to run from the Castle Keep to Amberley Castle, which is at least 3½ miles away. This has an involved story attached to it, which tells of a treasure of gold and silver plate belonging to the Cavaliers. This treasure was said to have been manhandled through the tunnel and then taken from Amberley by pack horse, and eventually buried in a deep well. A correspondent in the *West Sussex Gazette* (2 June 1966) told of how in 1906-8 a fellow boarder at his school had a tale of how his father took part in an attempt to send a greyhound from the Amberley end right through the tunnel to the Arundel entrance. This attempt failed, but later twenty rats were put in the tunnel and some of them were recaptured at the other end, proving that there was a way through.

There is an interesting story concerning tunnels that are said to run under the ruins of Slaugham Park. It seems there are two, one leading into a vault beneath the parish church, the other disappearing into the woods between Slaugham and Staplefield. These tunnels are supposed to be escape routes for an old Sussex family, the Coverts, either during religious persecution or during the struggle between Cavaliers and Roundheads. An unusual sidelight to the story is the claim that snow never lays on some patches of ground within the ruins. The theory is that the air contained in underground passageways beneath these spots keeps the ground above at a higher temperature. One local man recalled how his father had to stop working in the area, because his shovel would pass through the earth and into thin air. Other local stories speak of the ghost of a grey lady, and of Roman soldiers within the ruins.

Brighton may rival Arundel in its quantity of secret tunnels and passages. Many are said to run from the Pavilion, and it is conjectured that the Prince Regent caused the tunnels to be built when the Pavilion was for the use of himself and his friends. These passages are dealt with very well in Jeremy Errand's book, *Secret Passages and Hiding Places* (1974). He tells us that a passage still runs

Old print of Hastings' Caves, from a stereoscopic card sold in Hastings, at around the end of the last century.

under the lawn from the north end of the Pavilion, beneath the stables and the staff quarters, to emerge by means of a flight of steps in Church Street. It enabled the Prince to reach the stables in wet weather, although it may have been more of a curiosity than anything else. Other tunnel stories concerned with the Pavilion are of underground ways to a house in Hanover Crescent and other local houses. There is also a popular story of a passage to a house in the Old Steine, formerly the residence of Mrs Fitzherbert.

Other Brighton tunnel stories tell of an underground passage at Kemptown Slopes to beneath Marine Parade and of a secret passage from a hotel on King's Cliff to the sea-shore.

A well-documented Worthing story comes from 1959, when a local ophthalmic surgeon decided to have his waiting-room reconstructed. When the builders took up the floor they found a well-built underground passage with an arched ceiling. It was big enough for a person to wriggle into, although it only ran for about ten feet. The supposition was that it originally continued to a house near to the sea, which was formerly an inn, and which was always reputed to contain an underground tunnel. Smugglers were of course blamed for this underground activity. Before the new floor was laid, photographs were taken of the remains of the tunnel in Heene Road.

Apart from smugglers, the most often quoted reason for secret rooms and passages was that they were used by priests during the days of Catholic persecution. Slindon House is said to have more than one such hiding place. An interesting story concerning one of these hides tells of a priest who took refuge there during a determined search lasting for several days. When he finally left the hole, in his haste he caught his sleeve on a projecting nail, tearing a piece from it. The story of his escape was handed down in the family, including the account of the torn sleeve. In more recent times when the secret room was opened up, the fragment of cloth was still there.

It is said that many of the hide-holes in Sussex, made for use by priests, were the work of one Nicholas Owen, a Jesuit lay-brother, known to his friends as "Little John". Eventually he was tracked down and died under torture, refusing to the last to give details of any of his secret rooms.

One of the best known of the Priest's Holes is at West Grinstead, within the old prebystery next to the Catholic church. There seems some confusion concerning this hiding place and a secret chapel, which is visited by pilgrims from all over the world. The original priest's hole would almost certainly have been at the home of the much-persecuted Catholic family of Caryll, at West Grinstead House. The present priest's house with its hidden chapel is said to date from post-Elizabethan days, and it is therefore difficult to tie this in with the period of active Catholic persecution. But undoubtedly this house figures in the history of Catholicism in Sussex, and contains many interesting relics from past times, including a pewter chalice.

Slaugham Park under snow in 1952. It is here that some people claim it is possible to trace underground passages when snow covers the ground.

Buried Treasure

Anyone who has done a fair amount of walking in Sussex, particularly on the Downs and the coast, will tell you that it is not difficult to find treasure – perhaps not treasure of great material value, but things of beauty and interest nevertheless. On the Downs it may be possible to find flints, or one of the strange objects known as Shepherd's crowns, which when I was a schoolboy we called thunderbolts. On the beach there are pebbles of beauty, as well as lucky stones and the occasional coins. When my family moved into a new house in the 1930s, with a garden which had previously been meadowland, we dug up many coins going back to past centuries. No surprising, when we realized that the fields had been a favourite spot for travelling fairs.

But many kinds of treasure of far greater importance and value have been found. Some of the treasure stories are merely scraps of legends, repeated over and again, with little real substance, but others are more factual. The Cavaliers are often credited with leaving treasure in all sorts of places, such as Bosham and Amberley – but most villages have their treasure tales. Underneath the famous figure of the Long Man of Wilmington there is said to be a Roman in a gold coffin, and there is reputably treasure buried in a wood at Fittleworth. Chanctonbury Ring and Cisbury Ring are both known as treasure areas. Roman coins have indeed been found on Chanctonbury, and a treasure-filled passage is supposed to connect Cisbury Ring with Offington. A story has it that searchers began digging for it many years ago, but were driven off by large snakes who attacked the diggers with loud hisses.

Stories of treasure often precede a genuine find. Money Mound was the name given to a mound in Lower Beeding parish, north of Hammerpond Road. Rabbits had turned up coins, and in 1961 excavations took place, not primarily for treasure but for archaeological research. It was apparent that the site had already been inexpertly excavated in the 18th century, but nonetheless pottery fragments were found, as well as more coins. At the time I was given a jingle that neatly fitted the site and the year:

When the year is turned upside down,
Then treasure will be found in Money Mound.

Rather too neat to be genuine perhaps, and nobody seems to know exactly where the rhyme originated.

Even more romantic is the story of the Golden Calf that is supposed to have been brought to England by St Paul and buried in the centre of the Trundle at Goodwood. Whenever anyone tries to dig for the calf, the Devil moves it. A similar tale is told of other places in Sussex.

Tarberry Hill, near Harting, is said to be the resting place of treasure buried by the Royalists and left behind when they were surprised by Cromwell's men. Local rhymes have it that:

If Tarberry digged, were of gold should be the share.
or
Who knows what Tarberry would bear,
Must plough it with a golden share.

The magical word "gold" often features in these treasure stories, as the treasure itself – like the Golden Calf or the Knight in Golden Armour buried at Mount Caburn, near Lewes – or as the tool to be used by the treasure hunter.

Back to real treasure trove with a story from Selsey dating from 1925, when a Chichester governess walking along the shore spotted a golden glint in a heap of sand. It was a Celtic armlet of pure virgin gold, at least 2,000 years old and weighing

An old mug, which contained money, found in the chimney of a house in Horsham. The inscription reads "Hard very hard, the life of man is but a span but a woman life a yard".

Troves of Gold and Silver

over four ounces. It was known that an early British village was located nearby, so possibly this is not the only item of treasure waiting to be discovered.

One of the most exciting finds in Sussex was that of a farm labourer, who was ploughing on a farm at Mountfield in 1863. He unearthed a Celtic gold chain, which he took to be merely brass. He sold it at sixpence per pound to a man at Hastings, for five shillings and sixpence. The lucky (and obviously dishonest) purchaser sold it to a London dealer for £600, although its true value must have been much more. The Treasury heard of the find, but only after it had been melted down. The Hastings dealer and his London associate were each fined £265 for not reporting the treasure trove, but at least the original finder was allowed to hang on to his five and sixpence.

Another interesting find was a hoard of silver coins discovered at Washington in 1866. Years before, the locals had claimed to have seen a ghost of a Saxon knight, clad in chain mail, searching for something in the vicinity of an old barn. When the barn was eventually pulled down and the ground on which it stood ploughed up, the ploughshare cut into the jar containing the coins, which were thrown in all directions. It was said that the men of the village were happily exchanging coins for tankards of beer until the British Museum stepped in and claimed most of them. The old Saxon was apparently never seen again after the coins had been discovered.

When we think of treasure, we often imagine it in the proverbial treasure chest. One story which features such a chest concerns Herstmonceux Castle, which was said to be haunted by a demon drummer. One explanation for the sound of the drummer is that it was produced to frighten away those who might have been too inquisitive when the local smugglers were at work. In 1738 two lads at play found an old iron chest and two large hammers in an attic at the castle. When the chest was struck with the hammers it gave out a sound much like a kettle drum. The chest was supposed to have contained money and title deeds of great value, although after this find it seems to have disappeared. It came to light again in 1892, in an underground passage of the castle, but without any of the treasure.

Items found during excavations at Rusper Nunnery in the 19th century. The most interesting find was the enamelled chalice, which dates from the latter half of the 12th century.

Contraband

Sussex smugglers, with their apparently romantic background of brandy kegs, quietly moving convoys of laden pack-horses at the dead of night, and that little bit of baccy or spirits for those who had the sense to keep their mouths shut, constitute most people's mind picture of what this illegal operation was all about. No matter that the reality was often considerably less romantic, or even downright sordid – too many novelists and poets have written in rose-tinted terms about the trade of contraband for the picture to fade.

The last convoy of smuggled goods probably travelled through Horsham in about 1850. Earlier the movement of contraband through the town had been a thriving business, with many an apparently innocent load hiding goods of far greater value. By the middle of the 19th century this illicit trade had begun to decline because of the improved efficiency of the forces of law and order, and perhaps to some extent because of a change in social attitudes. But the town was to see just one more big smuggling operation, even if of a different kind, before such things became completely unknown.

Alfred and Dennett Allen were two brothers who had built up a successful business as maltsters and farmers. Alfred lived at Horsham, near his malthouse in Springfield Road. Dennett, the younger brother, lived at West Chiltington. They were a popular pair, both with their customers, to whom they sold their produce at reasonable prices, and with the farmers, from whom they purchased their stock at slightly higher rates than their competitors. They even paid good wages to their workers, something that was at that time sufficiently remarkable in itself. Even when other straight-dealing folk were finding trade difficult, the Allens continued to flourish. Further malthouses were added to the original ones at Horsham and West Chiltington, until eventually the business consisted of five warehouses, plus three farms.

But all was not right, and soon some of their competitors began to question seriously the matter of the Allens and their growing prosperity. Finally, in 1857, one of their workmen at Worthing, who along with many other members of the workforce had a pretty good idea of why things were going so well, threatened the brothers with exposure unless they agreed to finance him in his own business. Unwisely the Allens sacked him, whereupon he passed some of his inside knowledge to the excise authorities. Briefly, the situation was that the Allen brothers had been concealing roughly half the malt they purchased and reselling it without paying the government duty. This had been happening at each of the malthouses, although the one at Worthing was investigated first by the revenue men. Each store at Worthing was found to contain a secret vault, exactly equal in size to the legal one.

When news of the raid reached Horsham, the wagons were used that night to convey the smuggled malt housed in the Springfield Road secret vaults to Newbridge, where it was tipped into the river. During the days that followed local people rescued as much as they could and carried it away as pig food. It was said that a passage leading from the Horsham malthouse, running under Springfield Road and emerging in the meadow on the opposite side, was the route taken by the illegal malt on the start of its journey to Newbridge. The wagon wheels were wound with rope, to make them as silent as possible, although people living close-by must have had some idea of what was happening.

After Worthing, the excise officers searched all the Allen's warehouses, finding similar secret vaults

Far left: The hole made by one of the demolition men, after he realised that the apparently solid ground was in fact hollow. Photo: Mr C.W. Cramp

Left: Ron Lampard and Miss Joan Lampard, with Mr Lampard's son David, inspecting the tunnel leading from the Allen Brothers' vault. Photo: Mr C.W. Cramp

The Last Horsham Smugglers

at each. £12,000 worth of illegal malt was seized in these raids and taken to the Tower of London. The case was to be tried in London, but the Allens, realizing that the verdict would certainly go against them, fled the country on the day before the trial. They escaped to the United States, where, because of the lack of an extradition treaty, they were perfectly safe. They were fined £110,000 in their absence, but eventually the then solicitor general, realizing that there was no hope of getting this, agreed to reduce the fine to a mere £10,000. This the Allens paid and so were able to return home.

The story now moves forward by just over a century, to 1959, when the old Horsham gasworks was demolished. The works were just behind some shops on the east side of Springfield Road that had been the Allen brother's malthouse premises. During the demolition, a workman noticed that an apparently solid floor gave out a hollow sound. When he made a hole in the floor, he found first a vault underneath and then a tunnel leading towards the road. The passage, which was well built and dry, extended about 72ft, where it was blocked.

The full account of the Allens' illgotten empire is told in local historian William Albery's *A Millennium of Facts in the History of Horsham and Sussex 947-1947*, published in 1947, but the story of the tunnel beneath the road was not mentioned by him, although it had remained in local memories – as I found when several people told me about it. Mr Ernest Caplin, who lived in Springfield Road, had worked as a blacksmith in Horsham early in this century, and he remembered being told the story of the tunnel at that time, so the discovery in 1959 was no surprise to him or to his contemporaries.

I was able to go into the vault and make recordings there, talking to several of the people who lived nearby, and who had come to see the tunnel their fathers or grandfathers may have known something about. Apparently it had almost been rediscovered in about 1920, when part of an office floor had collapsed. I was told that the tunnel had other passages leading off it, although these could no longer be seen. And so the Allens' secret tunnel was finally sealed off and the last chapter in Horsham's smuggling history came to an end.

The remains in 1990 of the Allen Brothers' Malthouse building in Springfield Road, Horsham. Photo: C.W. Cramp

Trams and Trains

Our first unusual Sussex railway was certainly just that. Opened in 1895, it ran, on rails with the unusual gauge of 3 feet, from a terminus near Monkbretton Bridge at Rye to the Rye Golf Club, near Camber. As it was entirely on private land, no parliamentary powers were needed to open the railway, and because only one train ran on a single line, no signals were necessary.

The principal intention was for the Rye and Camber Tramway to transport golfers from the town of Rye to the golf course, but it was also used by local fishermen and holidaymakers, particularly after the line was extended to a new terminus just short of Camber, in 1908.

Colonel H.F. Stephens, who laid out the line, envisaged the railway working with some type of oil-powered locomotive. However, when it opened, it was with a conventional steam engine, which was given the name Camber. A second, similar but slightly bigger, locomotive was added in 1897; this was Victoria.

The passengers were accommodated in a bogie carriage, divided into first- and second-class sections by a partition. The first-class part boasted a clock and cushioned seats. The second-class section had sash windows, described as similar to windows in a house, and strip-wood seating. The windows could be completely removed in hot weather. Just before the arrival of the second locomotive, another passenger carriage was acquired. This was intended for third-class passengers only, and had three large windows on each side. There were also some goods wagons, which were used for carrying sand from Camber and, during World War I, for transporting ammunition. Eventually the two passenger coaches were rebuilt, and both ended up as third-class only.

In 1925 a four-wheeled petrol locomotive was acquired, which although not nearly as interesting-looking as the original steam engines, was in practical terms very successful. Later, poor old Victoria was sold for scrap, and Camber ended up in virtual retirement.

Incredibly the line weathered several financially difficult periods, and was still in use up to the start of World War II. At this time the tramway was requisitioned by the Admiralty and used to transport men and materials to a jetty that was being built on the Camber side of the river Rother, near the Golf Links station. (The second section of the line was not used by the Admiralty.) After the war, the line was returned to its former owners, but because both the track and the rolling stock were now in a fairly neglected state, it was decided to bring the undertaking to an end. And so this almost forgotten little Sussex railway, which had served its passengers for nearly fifty years, passed unnoticed into oblivion.

Our second line was much more of a real railway, although the Sussex novelist Sheila Kaye-Smith rather disparagingly called it a "toy" in her novel *Joanna Godden*. Its full title was the Hundred of Manhood and Selsey Tramway, but it was known to all who worked or travelled on it as the Selsey Bumper.

It functioned from 1897 to 1935 and ran the seven miles from Selsey Town Station to Chichester. There were eleven stations on the line, possibly a record for this distance on a standard-gauge railway.

Another brain-child of the ubiquitous Lieut-Colonel Stephens, it has passed into the folklore of the area, even being immortalized in song. The chorus of one such ditty ran: "The Sidlesham Snail, the Sidlesham Snail, the boiler's burst, she's off the

Far left: Victoria, one of the steam locomotives employed on the Rye and Camber Tramway. *Photo: Lens of Sutton*
Left: A pause at an unmanned crossing by a train on the West Sussex Railway, or to give it the more popular name The Selsey Tramway. *Photo: Mr J. Payne*

Three Unusual Railways

rail". But although the locals cursed its idiosyncrasies, it was also held in strong affection, and when in 1935 services were suspended many believed that it was only a matter of time before the railway would be reopened.

The rolling stock was of great interest to railway buffs. Over the whole period of the line's life it included seven different steam locomotives, bearing such local names as Selsey, Chichester, and Sidlesham. In 1928 petrol-engined rail cars were first used, and over the years this form of power, although less romantic than steam, proved economically successful. In 1932 it was stated that the cost of running had been reduced to 3.12 pence per mile, which was believed to be a world record. In comparison, a thirty-seater omnibus was said to cost ten pence per mile. The slogan was "ride on British-made steel instead of imported rubber". But, of course, the omnibus triumphed in the end.

The only one of our three little railways which is still running, and very successfully, is Volk's Electric Railway, which has been in existence at Brighton since 1883. The originator of this unique railway was a very remarkable man, Magnus Volk, who was born at Brighton in 1851. He was one of the fascinating band of Victorian inventors and among his interests were telegraphic instruments, street fire alarms, and electric light systems. In 1883 he successfully arranged the installation of electric light throughout the Royal Pavilion.

At about the same time he asked permission from the Brighton Corporation to run a short electric railway line on the sea front for a trial period of six months. A 2ft-gauge track was laid on the shingle, running about a quarter of a mile from near the Aquarium to the old Chain Pier. At the opening ceremony, the Mayor was carried in the first car, and the little railway proved so successful that the inventor obtained a further concession from the Corporation. Accordingly the gauge was changed to 2ft 9in, and the terminus became the Banjo Groyne. This involved a passage under the Chain Pier, and the line now became about three-quarters of a mile long, with a loop about half-way.

The rebuilt line opened in April 1884, and a regular service was then operated until 1940, apart from a few short interruptions. Of course, as with any railway, there were a number of minor accidents, and even one fatality, but most of the time the railway ran safely and efficiently.

When in 1940 the government closed the beaches because of the threat of German invasion, running the railway became impossible. After the war, although it was by that time in poor condition, it was decided to rebuild the track and restore the rolling stock. As visitors to Brighton well know, Mr Volk's electric railway still runs, and still attracts passengers. Both old friends of the line and newcomers are as fascinated by it as were their Victorian ancestors back in 1883.

Volk's Railway, the first electric railway in Sussex, when the railway ran out over the beach, instead of hugging the promenade as it does today.

Poor Man's Wall

Mention the Dyke, and most Sussex folk will immediately think of Devil's Dyke, near the village of Poynings on the Downs. "Dyke" is the Sussex dialect word for bank or earth wall. In modern times the word has come to mean the coombe or ditch, although the original dialect word for this would have been "Dick". An earlier popular name for Devil's Dyke was the Poor Man's Wall, Poor Man being one of the many names for the Devil.

The earthwork and the natural cleft in the Downs beside it have intrigued Sussex people through the ages. The well-known folk legend attached to it has already been told very briefly in the section of this book dealing with Old Scratch. The story has also been told several times in rhyme, and one of these attempts is on a postcard, copies of which were once sold on the site. An even better-known poem was written in 1798 by William Hamper and sold for twopence at Potter's Museum of Curiosities in Bramber. It concludes with the words, "Who dare now call the action evil, to hold a candle to the Devil?", a reference to the old dame who outwitted the Poor Man with her candle.

The area of the Devil's Dyke is now reasonably quiet and peaceful, apart from the cars whirling by on the Dyke Road, but this was not always the case. In 1901 T.C. Woodman wrote in his book *The South Downs*:

> *Thirty years ago this piece of the hills was the delight of every antiquary and every admirer of the South Downs... but thirty years is not now – everything is altered... at this once weird and secluded spot, hurrying crowds and noisy numbers are to be found daily where once were solitude and repose".*

Mr Woodman's ire was aroused by the entertainments and amusements that at the turn of the century were to be found over the whole of the Dyke area. It all began early in the 19th century when Tommy King, a Brighton musician, erected a wooden hut on wheels on the hill, in order to serve visitors with refreshments. Soon the hut was replaced by a small inn, which later grew into a hotel. After several landlords, Mr James Henry Hubbard came on the scene in 1892. He saw the possibilities of a spot that was becoming more and more popular with holiday crowds, brought out from Brighton by charabanc and train. Soon the fame of the Dyke spread to London, and excursion trains were bringing folk from the metropolis to add to the throng already taking advantage of Mr Hubbard's hospitality. The hotel itself was said to be the equal of any West End establishment, with a large coffee room, a smoking room, and an upstairs dining room. There was also a tearoom holding 200 people, and the amusements included all the usual paraphernalia of a fairground, plus a huge replica cannon, which featured on many of the picture postcards sold at the time.

Bands played on Sundays and Bank Holidays, and if this was not enough, those who wished could have their fortune told by Gypsy Lee, the Queen of the Gypsies.

Visitors to the Dyke did not have to depend on motor transport. In 1887 a railway line from Brighton to Devil's Dyke was opened by arrangement with the London, Brighton and South Coast Railway Company. It was a single track, leaving the Brighton-Portsmouth route half a mile beyond West Brighton station, and terminating at a little station 501 feet above sea level. The railway navvies excavating for the line unearthed the skeleton of a lady, with around her neck a string of precious stones. The navvies re-interred her bones, so she

Dyke Railway Station, the terminus of the Brighton-Dyke Railway, which operated from 1887 to 1938.
Photo: Mr I. Wale

was not examined by experts – who might have had something to say about her age. As it was, local folk were left to conjecture that the skeleton was of the old lady who had so successfully outwitted the Devil with her candle. What became of her necklace we are not told.

The success of the Dyke Railway was so great at the start that it surprised even its most fervent admirers. But the success was not maintained once the initial novelty had subsided, and by 1895 the railway was in real trouble and a receiver was appointed. This state of affairs continued until its incorporation into the Southern Railway in 1924. The line closed finally in 1938 – another victim of the motor car.

Strange as it may seem today, the branch railway line from Brighton to the Dyke was not the only railway associated with the spot during its period of manmade amusements. Our friend Mr Hubbard provided a double-track narrow-gauge steep-grade railway on the northern side of the Dyke hill in 1897. There were two cars, each seating twelve people. Like the conventional railway line, Hubbard's railway started auspiciously, being well patronized by visitors. But again the novelty must have worn off. By 1900 the line was put up for auction, but it was bought in because the bidding failed to reach the reserve of £390. The railway ceased to operate early in this century, and since then many walkers have been heard to conjecture about the original use of the strange metal shapes they stumble upon on the side of the hill.

Yet one more railway of sorts arrived at the Dyke when, in 1894, an aerial cableway was constructed across the ravine. There were two cars running on an endless cable, powered by an oil engine. The journey time one way was just over two minutes. This railway too, opened with a blast of publicity that ensured its initial success but then petered out. It ceased to operate early in the 1900s, and was used for target practice by troops during World War I. Perhaps, one may conclude, if there had been fewer mechanical marvels at the Dyke at the same time, some of them might have survived longer.

Mr Hubbard, who had such marvellous ideas for the Dyke, emigrated to Canada in 1907, and somehow nobody else saw things in quite the same light.

The Steep Grade Railway, once one of the three railways associated with the Dyke.

Scurrywinkle and Spirimawgus

I am sometimes asked, "Are there any Sussex dialect speakers left", although I suspect what the questioner really means is does anyone still speak with a Sussex accent. The answer is a very qualified yes. A number of Sussex folk, and not always the oldest, do still retain the attractive melodic cadence that seems to be peculiar to this part of England, but one hears it less and less. Dialect words and phrases are still used, but relatively rarely. We are all bombarded with standard English, interspersed with fashionable expressions, and to use a dialect word, which may not be understood, is almost a cause for shame, or at least embarrassment.

As a youngster I heard dialect and old-fashioned slang words and phrases used all the time, as I think my family were fairly slow to react to modern trends. Even today I find myself using words like spruser for someone who is a bit of a con man, or dorm when I actually mean to move slowly and clumsily. Somehow the standard words seem so much less descriptive than the old words I was brought up with. Although I would hesitate to use them in normal conversation, I can remember with satisfaction my parents coming out with scores of such words, such as dinlow (slow-witted), clung (half-dry), kiddie (mate or work-fellow), and puckered (snatched with cold).

There have been several Sussex dialect dictionaries published, and they make fascinating reading, not only as entertaining lists of unfamiliar words, but also as mirrors to the social life of past generations. But, in spite of the number of dialect words listed in dictionaries such as the Rev. William Douglas Parrish's (published in 1875, and expanded by Helena Hall in 1957), I am continually amazed by the number of words and phrases passed on to me by Sussex folk that have not been previously recorded.

Some of the most interesting are those with local connections. Mrs Jean Sunderland, a wonderful Sussex lady, who has given me so much from her vast store of traditional lore, told me how people once referred to "Campion's Eyebrows". These were the clumps of bushes on the north side of Wolstonbury Hill. (The Campion family owned the Elizabethan manor of Danny.) Jean Sunderland has shared with me many interesting dialect words and sentences. A slummocky person is an untidy character; tollard was the candle grease scraped out of the flat round candlesticks once in common use. Pook flies were the flies that in summertime, irritated the cows so much that they curled their tails over their backs and careered across the fields; only years later did Jean Sunderland realize that the old folk had been using an ancient word meaning puck – in other words these were fairy flies. When washing came out of the water with its colours streaked, it was said to have drented. One of her father's favourite phrases was, "Well, I'll go to Buxted Station"; a friend, when the sky looked stormy, would always come out with the remark, "Ah, it looks pretty black over Will's mother's"; the loft was always "Up in Annie's room".

The delight of many of these old expressions is that they give a glimpse of life as it was once lived in a slower, more peaceful age. "A regular honeypot of a lane" was a typical Sussex lane full of clinging mud. "So drunk, he couldn't see through a ladder" needs no explanation. "To fall there in twice" was to describe a very short distance. "Dull as ditchwater" meant exactly what it says, and equally "a month of Sundays" needs little explanation, when one remembers that Sunday in the country once meant a very quiet, even boring time for lively youngsters (at least that's how I remember it). A nice local expression "We'll go on the Linger and Die" meant the old steam line from Horsham to Steyning.

Before I leave words alone, here are some unusual ones given to me by Mr A.A. Moore. (He provided me with so many, that I can only select at random from among his riches.) A slouchpudden was a shambling walker; a brown George was a large apple turnover; scurrywinkle meant to move furtively or quickly; Old Spirimawgus was a name used for frightening naughty children (Devon dialect has Spirimogle, a supernatural being); a miriander was a happy halfwit (perhaps derived from "Merry Andrew"). "Layovers and catchmeddlers" was the reply to a nosey child who asked what were the contents of a bag or basket; "Easy as the boy knowed his father" was used when demonstrating something simple to a learner.

Regional and local words must have puzzled the folk who travelled around, but how much more interesting language was before it was standardized. Birds in Sussex were dishwipes (pied wagtails), Jacobs (starlings), tea leaves (siskins), and many more besides. People were often given nicknames, such as Fishy, Brasser, or Galloper, all completely descriptive of some aspect of their personalities, even if this was not immediately apparent to strangers. Villages even had their own rhymes, often in the form of jibes recited by those from neighbouring parishes:

Large parish, poor people,
Large new church, and no steeple.

This was one of the many people-and-steeple rhymes, it referred to East Grinstead.

Henfield was a market town,
When Brighton was a furzy-down

How much ruder can one get?

Lastly, two of my favourite Sussex proverbs: "One boy's a boy' two boys is half a boy; three boys is no boy at all" (which will be appreciated by anyone who has ever employed several boys to do a job), and "Everything in Sussex is a she, except a tom cat, and she's a he". In Sussex dialect speech, most things are termed "she", although I am unable to explain why.

Place names ending in "Ly" were always pronounced as "Lie" in Sussex. Hence the old riddle "three lies and all true?" The answer to which was three villages with names ending in "ly", such as Chiddingly, in this photograph from 1906.

Ballads and Riddles

Every county of England has these songs. They are traditional ballads that tell a story and at the same time hide a much deeper meaning. Songs full of this mixture of symbolism and the supernatural are an important part of our heritage of folklore, and in Sussex we are fortunate in having many of these strange and mysterious songs.

One of the oldest, and certainly one of the most interesting, is the song known as "The Bold Fisherman" or sometimes "The Young Fisherman". It is also sometimes referred to as "Down by the Riverside" (the second line of the words), but has absolutely no connection with an American song of this title. In 1908 Francis Jekyll and George Butterworth noted a version of this song from Mr Edmund Spooner, who was around 70, and an inmate of Midhurst workhouse. The singer told the two collectors that the song was "ancients of years old". The song has been sung by several traditional singers and collected by all the well-known collectors, such as Lucy Broadwood, although one would not term it a very common ballad. In 1956 Ken Stubbs noted a very similar version from George "Pop" Maynard of Copthorne. In 1967 I used to hear the marvellous old singer, George Belton of Madehurst near Arundel, very regularly. I had never heard him sing "The Bold Fisherman", so assumed it was not in his repertoire. One week, another singer sang it (in this case learnt from a published source) and George confided to me afterwards that he knew the song, although he had not sung it for several years. The very next time we met, George had dredged up this fine song from the recesses of his memory, and was able to perform a very complete version of it. I later recorded it for an LP record, so he never had the chance to forget it again.

The song tells the story of a fisherman, who allows a girl to see that he is no ordinary man, but is in fact a "Lord" wearing three chains of gold. She is frightened that she has offended him by not recognizing his nobility, but he assures her that she has in no way spoilt her chances of becoming his bride. Because of the obvious age of the song, students of folklore believe that the song may well refer to the "fisher of men" (Jesus Christ) or even to an older Saviour from pre-Christian times.

Most traditional singers who know this song have no idea of these fascinating conjectures, and to them it is just another song, no older or of any more importance than a Victorian tear-jerker that may also be part of their repertoire. In this respect it is interesting that Mr Spooner in 1908 spoke of the song with so much reverence regarding its age.

Also of considerable age are the riddle songs, which are found all over the British Isles, and indeed in other parts of the world. A fairly common one is "Sing Ivy" or "An Acre of Land". This is a simple list of tasks performed in a seemingly impossible manner – the acre of land is ploughed with a ram's horn, cut with a pen knife, measured by thimbleful, etc. What this seems to be is a much attenuated version of a longer song known as "The Elfin Knight". This is the archetype of courtship songs where the suitor is expected to perform a number of strange or impossible tasks. These songs merge into the straightforward riddle songs, the best known being "I Will Give My Love a Cherry [or Apple]". Charlie Potter sang me a typical version of "Sing Ivy" in 1956. He was recalling for me some of the songs he remembered hearing from old Henry Burstow (Horsham's celebrated song man, who knew between 400 and 500 songs) as they had been sung to his father, as the two men sat at the kitchen table, with young Charlie taking it all in,

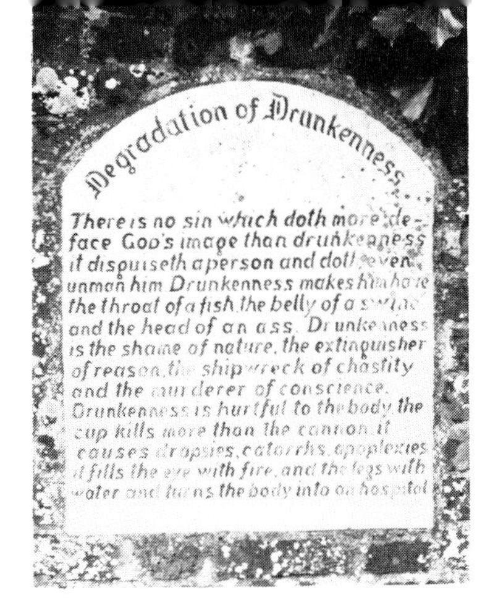

Left: Declaration against drunkenness which can be seen on a wall at Kirdford in West Sussex.
Far left: Michael Turner, Warnham's Grand old man who was not only Parish Clerk and Sexton, but also a celebrated fiddler and singer.

underneath the table. "Sing Ivy", though, was a song that he had learnt from his father; it was not one of Henry Burstow's.

The riddle songs will be known to many people – one even provided the tune for a pop song, "The First of Never". My own particular favourite is "Piri-iri-igdum", which I learnt from my mother, who in turn had learnt it from her mother, who had learnt it from her father. Like the other riddle songs, it includes a number of unusual presents, such as a chicken without a bone and a cherry without a stone. The supernatural element of "The Elfin Knight" is missing, although the way the riddles are explained is far from commonplace.

We could look at several other magical songs, but one more must suffice. This is the very lovely "The Seeds of Love", sometimes called "Sowing the Seeds of Love". This song seems to be connected with the similar "The Sprig of Thyme", although the latter is considered the older of the two. In these songs the imagery of plants and flowers is used in a very delicate way, to express thoughts that perhaps in more mundane words would be considered indelicate. The version I have sung for many years I originally learnt from another singer, who said that it was as sung by Burstow, and as such I have introduced the song whenever I have trotted it out in public. Recently I came across the printed copy of his "Seeds of Love" noted from him in 1893 by Lucy Broadwood. I now find that his version is much nearer to "The Sprig of Thyme" song, and nothing like the one I sing. I can only console myself that perhaps he knew both versions.

Henry Burstow. As well as a notable bell-ringer and walker, he knew around 500 songs, many of which were noted down by folk song collectors such as Lucy Broadwood and Ralph Vaughan Williams.

Christmas Past

Christmas is a time for looking back. Somehow Christmas days of the past appear more enjoyable, more special, and indeed more magic, than those of the present. Recalling my own boyhood, I can call up with affection the thrill of receiving a penny-stamped postcard from my grandmother living in Littlehampton, telling us to pick up a parcel at the Southdown bus office. (This was in the days when it was cheaper to send a parcel by bus for a short distance than to use the post.) When we picked up granny's parcel it was, as expected, bulging with inexpensive but exciting goodies for each member of the family. Granny's Christmas parcel was definitely an important part of my childhood Christmas. Then there was the unaccustomed experience of being put to bed around teatime on Christmas Eve, only to be roused again later in the evening. After a lukewarm flannel had been gently rubbed over my face, I was dressed in my warmest clothes for the mile-long walk to midnight mass. What a magical experience! After all the excitement of Christmas Day, there was an almost equally important day to follow. Boxing Day was the occasion of our annual visit to my great-uncle and great-aunt in the country. We travelled by double-decker bus (an event in itself) to their apple-scented house, where spring water was pumped straight into the kitchen sink. My uncle entertained us with simple tricks and jokes (the same every year), and after a meal I was allowed to accompany the adult males as they set out on a very masculine expedition, with my uncle carrying his gun. I was even allowed to fire it once; an event that made that particular Boxing Day even more special than usual. After tea, we stood outside the drive to my uncle's house waiting for the bus, my uncle holding a hurricane lamp to ensure that the bus stopped to pick us up. Oh the importance of it all!

Christmas time in Sussex many years before must have been spartan by modern standards, at least for the working population. Probably only Christmas Day itself was very much different to all the rest of the year, and even that was not very exceptional. The several Sussex diarists do not tell us much about Christmas, so we can only conclude that nothing very notable took place. We do hear of the custom of farmers inviting their workmen to the farmhouse to partake of Christmas dinner, and this was probably the only way in which the day was marked as being slightly out of the ordinary. One farmer's Christmas dinner of 1706 included plumm pottage, calf's head and bacon, goose, pig, roast beef, veal, two baked puddings, and minced pies.

Plumm pottage was the forerunner of our familiar Christmas pudding. It was eaten at the start of the meal, and was a mixture of sweet and savory ingredients, such as beef, currants, raisins, prunes, sugar, claret, and lemon-juice – all thickened with bread or sago into a sort of thick broth.

Mincemeat, too, was, even up to a century ago, made with real meat, as well as the more familiar currants, peel, and apples. In Sussex mince-pies were never made in a round shape. Even in 1944 a contributor to *Sussex Notes and Queries* said he knew of an old Newhaven lady who declared that "It isn't Christian" when her daughter proposed to bake a mince-pie in a new-fangled round tin. The shape had to be a long oval, to represent the manger at Bethlehem. The ingredients, which if possible should include a little smuggled brandy, were sometimes said to represent the gifts of the Three Kings.

One particular Christmas ritual in Sussex,

Left: Kings Road, St Leonards, looking towards Warrior St railway station. The date is early 1900s.

Below: December 30, 1908 in Bognor. All the elements of a typical Christmas scene with postmen ankle-deep in snow.
Photo: Mr J. Sykes

When Mincemeat was Mince Meat

which must go back a very long way, is the burning of the yule log, which had to continue until Twelfth Night. When it was finally extinguished, a piece of the log was carefully retained, to assist in the lighting of the next yule log. Thus the continuity of good luck engendered by the annual burning of the log was ensured. There are several other superstitions attached to the Christmas log. If a person with a squint, or one who is barefooted, comes to the house during the period it is burning, then bad luck will undoubtedly follow.

The wassail bowl included a mixture of wines, spiced, and sweetened with apples bobbing about on the surface. Sometimes ale would be used, with nutmeg, sugar, and ginger. A popular name for this drink in Sussex was "lamb's wool", and I am sure it was particularly appreciated by the Downland shepherds when they came in from their cold work.

We saw a change taking place in Christmas, as in many other things, during Victorian days. Foreign customs such as the Christmas tree, and a different kind of Father Christmas, become popular. And for at least one day in the year even the most humble country folk enjoyed something approaching plenty. The Christmas pudding is typical of the Victorian Christmas, and it soon had its own traditions and customs, just as the older Christmas fare. The last Sunday before Advent was "Stir-up Sunday", when Sussex housewives made and stirred their puddings. All the family had to take a turn in stirring, making a wish as they did so. The spoon had to be made of wood (because the Bethlehem manger was of wood) and it had to be turned from left to right, the way the Three Kings travelled when they followed the star. Failure to follow these rules would, of course, bring bad luck to the house.

One Sussex custom that went back a long way, and yet lingered on even into the early years of this century, was the charming observance of "Going-a-Gooding". This was always done on St Thomas' Day (21 December) and consisted of the older and poorer ladies presenting themselves at the doors of the big houses, where they were invariably given gifts of money, or in kind, to help them enjoy their Christmas. There are many delightful stories attached to this custom. The vicar of Upper Beeding in the early years of the 19th century was in the habit on 21 December of sitting at his study window with a pile of silver coins in front of him. The old ladies of the village would curtsy to thank him as they received their "dole". Henry Burstow, in his *Reminiscences of Horsham* (1811), tells us about Gooding Day, although surprisingly he attaches it to 26 December – surely a slip, as all other Sussex references tell us that it was 21 December. Lady Hurst noted the custom in 1889, when she commented on the "pretty sight" of old people with scarlet cloaks and black satin bonnets receiving their gifts. Landowners would change a considerable sum into silver coins, giving anything from sixpence to half-a-crown to those whom they felt deserved it. It was customary to give widows double the amount given to others.

BIBLIOGRAPHY

Albery, William, *A Millenium of Facts in the History of Horsham and Sussex*, 1947.
Baldwin, B. Marjorie, *The Story of the Forest*, 2nd edition, 1985
Beckett, Arthur, *Adventures of a Quiet Man*, 1933
The Spirit of the Downs, 1909
The Wonderful Weald, 1911
Bentley, J.H., *Copthorne People and Places*
Blaker, N.P., *Sussex in Bygone Days*, 1919
Broadwood, Lucy E., *English Traditional Songs and Carols*, 1908
Brown, L.E., *All About Bury*, 1948
Burstow, Henry, *Reminiscences of Horsham*, 1911
Butterworth, George, *The Ploughman's Glory*, 1977
Candlin, Lillian, *Memories of Old Sussex*, 1987
Carley, Gaius, *Memoirs*, 1963
Clark, Paul, *The Railways of Devil's Dyke*, 1976
Cook, C.F. (Ed.), *Another Book of Sussex Verse*, 1928
Copper, Bob, *Early to Rise*
Cosby, Iris, *Withyam, Sussex*, 1977
Dale, Anthony, *Brighton Town and Brighton People*, 1976
Dean-Smith, Margaret, *A Guide to English Folk Song Collections 1822-1952*, 1954
De Candole, Henry, *The Story of Henfield*, 1976
Errand, Jeremy, *Secret Passages and Hiding Places*, 1974
Fryer, Norman (Ed.), *Natural History of St Leonard's Forest*
Grant, L., *A Chronicle of Rye*, 1926
Grantham, W.W., *Stoolball and How to Play It*, 1919
Greenfield, J.O., *Tales of Old Petworth*, 1976
Griffith, Edward, *The Selsey Tramways*, 1974
Hall, Helena, *Lindfield, Past and Present*, 1960
Halsham, John, *Idlehurst*, 1898
Harding, Peter A., *The Rye and Camber Tramway*, 1985
Hare, Augustus, *Sussex*, 1894
Holman, G., *Sussex*, 1894
Hurst, Lady Dorothea E., *Horsham: Its History and Antiquities*, 1868
The History and Antiquities of Horsham, 2nd edition, 1889
Jackson, Alan A., *Volk's Railway, Brighton*
Johnson, Walter, *Talks with Shepherds*, 1925
Lee, Barbara, *Groombridge Old and New*, 1978
Leigh, J., *Past and Passing*, 1932
Lucas, E.V., *Highways and Byways in Sussex*, 1904
Manville, Sid, *Everything Seems Smaller*, 1989
McCann, Timothy J., *West Grinstead: A Centre of Catholicism in Sussex, 1671-1814*, 1987
Merrifield, R., *"Good Friday Customs in Sussex" (Sussex Archaeological Collections*, Vol. LXXXIX, 1950)
Meynell, Esther, *Sussex*
Middleton, Judy, *A History of Hove*, 1979
Migood, F.W.H., (Ed.) *Worthing: A Survey of Times Past and Present*, 1938
Moore, Giles, *The Journals of Giles Moore 1656-1679*
Pagden, Florence A., *A History of Alfriston*, 1899
Parish, Rev. W.D., *A Dictionary of Sussex Dialect*, 1875
Rees, Josephine Duggan, *Portrait of Slindon*, 1969
Ridley, U., *The Story of a Forest Village*, 1971
Robinson, Audrey M., *Shelley: His Links with Horsham and Warnham*, 1983
Scott, Hardiman, *Secret Sussex*, 1949
Simpson, J. *British Dragons*, 1980
Folklore of Sussex, 1973
Smith, Henry J., and Charman, Aubrey, *History of Southwater*, 1977
Staines, Rev. E.N., *Dear Amberley*, 1968
Straker, Ernest, *Wealden Iron*, 1931
Stubbs, Ken, *The Life of a Man*, 1970
Taylor, James, *The Sussex Garland*, 1851
Walker, Peggy, *Rudgwick Memories*, 1982
Wolseley, Viscountess, *The Countryman's Log Book*, 1921
Woodman, T.C., *The South Downs*, 1901
Woodward, Marcus, *Mistresss of Stanton's Farm*, 1938
Young, Colonel A. Donovan, *Titus Oates Lived Here*, 1958